BEWARE...

You are about to  w what one of those is, then per a form of puzzle book in which the rnity. It is an escape room in th wn path, but your route is often ... you give to the puzzles you encounter along the ....y. You must solve the puzzles to escape the pages.

Some puzzles will offer you alternative routes according to your solution. Others will invite you to calculate the next entry you should turn to. When this happens, you should check the 'from' number to ensure that you came from the right location and are still on the right path. If you find that you have arrived from the wrong place, you should turn back and think again.

Not all wrong solutions will end the story. As befits an adventure in which you play the role of Sherlock Holmes, this book is far more cunning than that. Some wrong answers may have unforeseen consequences further down the path, causing you to miss a helpful clue or even land a red herring.

While you are trapped inside the Escape Book, you should pay attention to everything you see. Once the game is afoot, there are all manner of clues hidden on the pages. Use Watson's Notebook – which you will discover shortly – to record your observations. Some of these notes might be needed to solve later puzzles. You will also be required to master the Translation Device, located on the cover of the book (of which, more later). If you are struggling with your art of deduction, you will find some helpful hints and clues (and even the answers) located at 221A and 221B, found at the back of the book.

There is more than one door through which you can exit the Escape Book. Some doors are marked with triumph... others with infamy. Only the most observant of detectives will find an escape route that results in newspaper headlines proclaiming their heroic success.

▶ *These arrows direct you to your next entry.*
Now, all great adventures begin by turning the first page...

WATSON'S NOTEBOOK

Use this notebook to jot down anything of interest you encounter during your adventure; you may find it helps you to solve a later puzzle.

NOTES & OBSERVATIONS

I brought along my Morse code notes.
(These can be found at the back of the book.)

▶ *If you have yet to begin your adventure – Turn over the page*
(Feel free to refer to Watson's Notebook at any time.)

THE STORY

In the upcoming adventure, you will take on the role of the world's most famous consulting detective, Sherlock Holmes, as he becomes trapped within a dastardly plot. You will see everything from his point of view, you will attempt to solve the puzzles with his powers of deduction, you will be him! You might even find a magnifying glass helpful. So, try to think in the way that Sherlock thinks. As he once said, in Sir Arthur Conan Doyle's *The Sign of the Four* (1890): "When you have eliminated the impossible, whatever remains, HOWEVER IMPROBABLE, must be the truth."

You will be accompanied, of course, by your faithful companion Doctor John H. Watson. He will offer you words of advice, a voice of reason and a steady hand in times of peril. You should also make good use of his notebook to record observations that may help with your escape.

This adventure is set in the British Museum on a wintry spring afternoon and night in 1901, a few weeks after the death of Queen Victoria on 22 January that year. The country has its first new monarch, in King Edward VII, for more than 63 years. He has acceded to the throne, but he is yet to be crowned king. And so Great Britain and its vast worldwide empire are in a time of flux – might groups set on disrupting the status quo see this as an opportune moment to strike at the heart of the Establishment?

Many of the objects described in these pages can still be seen in the British Museum, including the Rosetta Stone, the Elgin Marbles and the giant granite head of Egyptian ruler Amenhotep III. The map you will be given is based on a genuine floor plan of the Museum from this period. Today, some of the Museum rooms have been rearranged – the large Reading Room has been closed and its thousands of volumes have been moved to the British Library. In others, such as the vast and beautiful Enlightenment Gallery (in this era called the King's Library), you will today be able to revisit the scenes of this tale. The British Museum Underground Station, which features in this adventure, was open to serve Museum visitors from 1900 to 1933.

Good luck – keep your wits about you! The game is afoot.

THE TRANSLATION DEVICE

Set into the cover of the Escape Book is a Translation Device, which is an essential part of your equipment for solving some of the puzzles you will encounter. It features a series of windows behind which are letters, numbers, colours, and a sequence of hieroglyphs and other linguistic marks. These can be used in a number of ways:

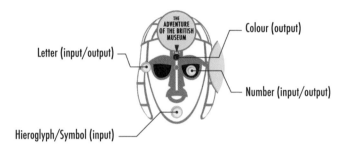

You can find a digital version of the Translation Device at:
www.ammonitepress.com/gift/sherlock-translation-device/

In some puzzles you'll discover coded messages in the form of strings of random numbers or secret symbols hidden in the story. Using the Translation Device, input your discoveries in the relevant *input* dial, then decode them by reading the relevant *output* dial.

You may recognize the celebrated helmet into which the Translation Device is fitted on the cover of this book. This is sadly not an artefact that Sherlock and Doctor Watson could have enjoyed viewing at the Museum because it was not found until 1939. But one fact about its discovery makes it rather suitable for inclusion in this book. Can you work out why? Look at the other information on the book's cover. (Need help? Turn to the Hints section at the back of the book.) If you've solved the puzzle, please send us a message:
#SherlockHolmesEscapeBook @ammonitepress

▶ *If you are ready to begin your adventure – Turn to 1*

EGYPTIAN CENTRAL SALOON

The shadows are lengthening in the British Museum. The rain splatters against the window of the Egyptian Central Saloon. Outside, the wind is howling.

"Weather's taken a turn for the worse, Holmes," says Watson. "Nasty."

"Hmm," you say.

There's hardly anyone about. It is only a few minutes from closing time.

"We'd better make a move, old man," Watson mutters. "Rainstorm or no rainstorm."

"Hmm," you repeat.

A minute or two passes. You are moving slowly between the exhibits, Watson trailing behind you. You feel you are close to a breakthrough in a case that the world would come to know as the Conk-Singleton Forgery. In your hand you clutch a letter. It has a message in a language that looks a little like the hieroglyphs and other linguistic marks found on the famous Rosetta Stone. It is this letter that has brought you to the Museum, and here to the Egyptian Central Saloon.

"I was surprised you wanted to come here after what you said yesterday," Watson says.

"What was that?"

"That you felt absolutely no inclination to help the assistant director despite his many letters."

"And three telegrams, Watson, if you remember."

The assistant director of the British Museum, Sir Alisdair Stuart, has been contacting you daily, requesting your presence at an 'urgent meeting' in the Museum. You had something of a falling out with him last year and have resisted his requests.

"Well, we're not here to help him, Watson. We're here because this fascinating letter came in the lunchtime post. And I'm sure these hieroglyphs and their arrangement hold a clue as to where to go next."

You show the paper to Watson once again.

▶ *Study the note carefully – Turn to 91*

My dear Mr Holmes,

    You must look for a Stone in the middle of Egypt. For the king is in danger.

    You will be trapped. Can you translate your suffering into glory and save the ruler when he goes underground?

    But be careful! Is there forgery afoot?

In freedom,

Lady Arabella Conk-Singleton

② THE ATTENDANT'S IDENTITY

"Holmes, the Diogenes Club is Mycroft's club, I believe... And the letter mentions your brother... Could he be involved in whatever scheme we are embroiled in?"

"We shall see."

"Thinking of Moriarty, I've just realized who that wretched attendant reminded me of!"

"Who?"

"Sebastian Moran, that's who! Moriarty's right-hand man. The person you yourself described as the second most dangerous man in London."

"Yes, I saw that straight away."

"But how, Holmes?"

"My name is Sherlock Holmes," you say. "It is my business to know what other people don't."

Watson makes a note of the phrase. Sometimes he is a trifle too keen.

"Well, if it is Moran, he must have an ally," Watson continues. "His is not the kind of mind to dream up a plot like this..."

"Observe the bottom of the invitation, Watson," you say, narrowing your eyes. "There are some scribbled numbers."

M. Napoleon requests the pleasure of the company of Sir Edward Maunde Thompson, museum director, and assistant director Sir Alisdair Stuart in the Stranger's Room at the Diogenes Club.

20 – 8 – 5 / 2 – 1 – 18 – 4

"What could that mean, d'you think, Holmes?"

"A number to letter code, clearly. They have provided the last letter."

"Well, we can't use the Translation Device here, because the letter 'D' does not correspond with the number '4' on that," Watson says.

"But look, there seem to be some letters underlined in the invitation." You work out what it spells.

▶ *It spells THE BARD – Turn to 113*

▶ *It spells THE DEAD – Turn to 53*

▶ *It spells TWO FLED – Turn to 92*

③ THE TRANSLATION DEVICE

"Well, how can you use this pattern with the Translation Device?" Watson seems almost belligerent, as he often does when baffled.

"The pattern seems to match the layout of the symbols and hieroglyphs in the letter. Agreed?"

"Yes."

"My idea is to transcribe the hieroglyphs and letters into numbers."

Watson seems to be warming to the task. "I wonder about these addition signs... Add twice?"

Using your Translation Device, convert the symbols and hieroglyphs from Lady Arabella's letter into numbers. Add up the numbers, then add the digits together.

▶ *Turn to the number you discover*

④ A SUDDEN SUMMONS

"4," Watson says, tapping the paper. "Now where is item 4?" He pauses. "Holmes, I think it might be the Ros–"

Suddenly, there is a commotion.

"What the devil?" Watson exclaims.

A young man comes hurtling down the centre of the Saloon, heading straight towards you.

He arrives, panting. "Holmes, Mr Holmes!" He stops and bends over, gasping for air. The chap looks like an office clerk and clearly isn't used to exercise.

"Mr Holmes," he says, regaining his composure, "the assistant director is in need of you in the Trustees' Room."

You look at him, quizzically.

"He asked for you and sent me here," the young man says, in an attempt to answer your unspoken question.

"How the deuce did he know you were here, old man?" says Watson.

"Intriguing," you say. "But I am busy with an important case in the Egyptology department. Please send my apologies."

You turn back to the exhibit in front of you, *The Egyptian Book of the Dead*. He doesn't leave.

"Please, sir, he is in urgent need."

Do you follow him?

▶ *Yes – Turn to 71*

▶ *No – Turn to 30*

⑤ EPHESUS ROOM

You turn towards the Ephesus Room, and for a moment think that you can see a broom disappearing into the darkness. Ahead, there are arrows on the floor. However, the arrows have heads pointing in both directions, and as you follow one towards a sculpture you notice scrape marks on the floor, suggesting it has been pulled into the centre of the room from a position against the far wall.

Watson strikes a match and holds it up to the sculpture. "Part of a column from the Temple of Artemis at Ephesus. Showing a human figure, thought to be Eurydice, standing next to Death."

"There's another code here, Holmes. HEUR.3TY and there are those letters again, IAN."

You take note of the code; it might prove useful later.

Moving the match slightly, Watson illuminates some numbers chalked on the floor by the statue:

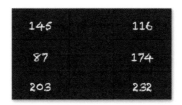

And there is a note, which he reads aloud: "What divides us? Beware what lies ahead. To go forward is odd, to retrace your steps is even now possible. If you fail there will be nothing remaining of your reputation."

"What divides us?" Watson muses. "It's clearly a number puzzle."

"Perhaps a number that divides into all of them?"

You set to work.

▶ *If you get an even number, go back to the*
Archaic Room – Turn to 13

▶ *If you get an odd number, go forward to the*
Elgin Room – Turn to 11

⑥ OUTSIDE THE DIRECTOR'S OFFICE

You make your way to Room 6 on the map, the Director's Office. Just outside the office you see something moving out of the corner of your eye. You turn, and think you might have seen a chap with a broom moving back into the darkness. You blink... but nothing.

In front of you is a beautiful statue of Venus. It seems to have been moved from its correct position.

"I say, Holmes, is there something significant about this?" Watson asks.

He is pointing at the item code, which has been circled in pencil with the letters IAN written below:

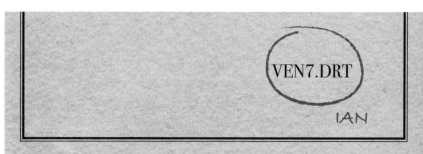

You make a note of the code in the notebook in the hope that it might be useful later.

As you straighten up, you hear a rattling of keys by the main Museum entrance. You hear someone swinging the great door shut with a bang and then the sound of them locking it and rattling the keys with relish.

"What was that?" Watson asks.

"We're locked in," you say.

"Locked in, Holmes?" Watson squawks. "Oh Lord, this is a disaster. What is that wretched fellow playing at?"

"Come on," you soothe, "no need for panic. What's become of your military backbone? There's only one way out of here and that's to play the game."

▶ *Turn to 26*

"7," you say. "Get out the map, Watson. Room 7 – where are we headed?"

Watson pulls the map from his pocket and scans it.

"There's no Room 7, Holmes," Watson says, scratching his beard.

"But there's a bookcase 7," you say, pointing at the far wall.

Watson follows your finger.

"Brilliant as ever, Holmes."

You walk over. In the centre of the bookcase, a single book has been pulled out slightly. On its spine are printed the words 'Sherlock Holmes'.

"That book has your name on it!" Watson chuckles, tickled by his own joke.

You sigh pointedly, pull the book out and turn to page 7. On page 7 you see two symbols. The symbols remind you of something you saw earlier that day. You pull it from your pocket and line it up. Together, they make a sequence.

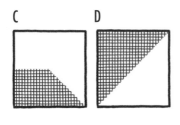

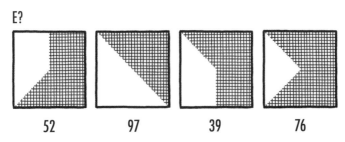

| 52 | 97 | 39 | 76 |

▶ *Find the start of the sequence, then solve 'E' – Turn to your answer*

THE ADVENTURE OF THE BRITISH MUSEUM

⑧ A VERY INTELLIGENT FLY

You look around for item 8.

"Here, Holmes." Watson is pointing to a model boat with a crew of oarsmen.

"From a tomb, I suppose?"

In place of one of the figures there is a curled note.

"Bella Rabia!"

"Didn't we have a news clipping about her?"

"She is behind this! Good Lord, Holmes! One of the most intelligent women of her generation? The king is done for! And we're stuck here..."

▶ *If you'd like to consult the newspaper clipping concerning Bella Rabia – Turn to 29, then return here*

▶ *Turn to 78*

My dear and most brilliant Mr Holmes and his shuffling associate,

I and my comrades in the London Anarchists Group have been trying to alert you to a major crisis – a regicide. We call ourselves the Bonapartists.

I arranged for my comrade Sir Alisdair Stuart to lure you to the Museum, but you would not come.

Now you are trapped like a fly in a dish of ointment.

A very intelligent fly, I must admit, since you have found your way to this letter.

I take delight in informing you that the Rosetta Stone you are looking at is a forgery – the original is in a case at London Docks ready to cross the Atlantic to Texas. The thousands of pounds sterling Sir Alisdair received for it are sitting in our coffers.

It seems appropriate that the Stone found by Napoleon Bonaparte's men in Egypt should fund the next great adventure of the Bonapartists.

On the forged Stone I took the liberty of getting the forger to add a message to you – which must have led you here. A nice touch, I thought?

Now you are trapped here, in a cage of our design.

Unless you can escape the Museum before tomorrow morning at 9 a.m. you will be unable to stop our Greatest Act of Violence yet – the assassination of the king.

A first step towards ushering Anarchy into the United Kingdom. We will be subject neither to gods nor men.

We are not monsters, though. I respect the human brain and am determined we should give you a chance to stop the plot.

Your only chance is to get to the end of the route we have laid down for you through the Museum.

Before tomorrow morning at 9.

Next, a sinister clue: head upcountry.

Yours,
Bella Rabia

⑨ IN THE MUSEUM COURTYARD

from 41, 72

You look back at the Museum frontage.

"I say," Watson murmurs. "Look at that! Someone's been up to some strange tricks. Why would anyone have done that?"

You look around for the attendant. But he seems to have melted into the shadows.

"Curious fellow... What a ridiculous appearance," Watson says, rather too loudly.

Is Watson scared? you wonder.

"A disguise, definitely," you say. "But what is he trying to hide? He could have done better than that atrocious Scottish accent, too!"

"Another thing, Holmes – isn't the Museum supposed to be closed for the afternoon? Why is there a light flashing in the window there?"

"Perhaps things are not so quiet within as we thought."

"There's something familiar about that pattern, Holmes..." Watson muses aloud. "I feel like I've seen it somewhere today."

You look at the Conk-Singleton letter and the papers you gathered from the doctor.

Do you see a connection with the pattern on the front of the Museum?

▶ *If you see a connection with the letter – Turn to 79*

▶ *If you see a connection with the map – Turn to 99*

THE MEN OF LEWIS

from 77

You hurry along a small corridor.

"Holmes, we are running out of time!" Watson puffs behind you.

"I know," you reply, perhaps a little too curtly. The pressure appears to be getting the better of you.

Together, you stumble into a small room. The walls are lined with glass cases. Metal plates and armour shine from within.

"The Mediaeval Room," Watson says, pointing at a sign just above your head.

"Indeed, Watson," you respond, rather exasperatedly. You'd mentally dated the artefacts on entry.

Watson taps his head. "Between the fifth and the fifteenth," he says, then looks at you. "The Mediaeval period – that was between the fifth and fifteenth centuries!"

"Focus, Watson," you say. "What are we looking for?"

Your eyes quickly scan the room, looking for something out of place, and land on the two large glass cabinets in front of you. One of the doors is slightly ajar.

"See here, Watson," you say, walking over. You look through the glass and you're surprised to see below...

"A game of chess!" Watson exclaims as he joins you. "Of course, the Lewis chessmen!"

You look at the board and the figures sitting on it.

"Something's not quite right, Watson," you say.

You peer closer. Around the edge you can see a handwritten scrawl:

Figure low faces figure high, each of them back to back.
The crown, we know, is soon to die, and from behind comes the attack.
Who is the killer?

"Some sort of old proverb," says Watson, wandering off.

"No, Watson, he's talking about the plot! But come, look at these pieces."

There are four chess pieces sitting in the centre of the chessboard in a straight line.

"They're not as they should be," you say. "No game would create a board that looks like this."

"And this last question, too," you wonder. "Who is the killer?"

"Well, the anarchist obviously," Watson says. His voice seems distant.

"Mmm, indeed, yes," you hear yourself respond. You are lost on the board again, grappling with the puzzle, as the minutes tick away.

Enter the first and then the last letter of the killer's name into the Translation Device and take note of the two-digit number.

▶ *Turn to the number you discover*

(11) ELGIN MARBLES

"Now we've been sent to the Elgin Marbles, Holmes. Rather beautiful."

"Although it's a shame to see them here, old chap, rather than on the Acropolis."

Watson ponders your comment.

"Look at this, Watson."

You're pointing towards one section of the Elgin Marbles. There are a few things out of place.

If you so wish, you may decide to make a note of the items in Watson's Notebook (found at the front of the book).

"What is the point of the black flag?"

"Let's have a look at the letter from Bonaparte again, Watson. It says 'Would you say you were an anarchist, Mr Holmes? A hater of authority? A violent man? By the time this night has ended I predict you will be seen in that light by the powers that be. Even by your brother. You will be shamed.'"

"Look at the arrangement, Holmes. A collapsed figure wearing a crown. A seated man holding a gun."

"An assassination you might think..."

"Of a king... A regicide."

"And what about this black flag?"

"Well, I'm guessing anarchism, Holmes. The black flag is the anarchist flag, what?"

"Intriguing, yes, intriguing."

You both stand there in silence, stunned.

▶ *Turn to 56*

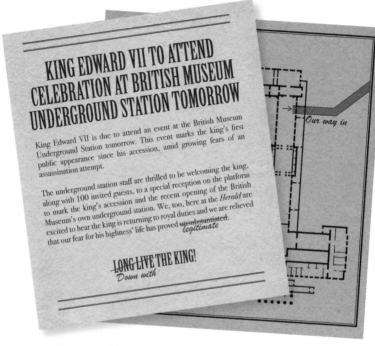

KING EDWARD VII TO ATTEND
CELEBRATION AT BRITISH MUSEUM
UNDERGROUND STATION TOMORROW

King Edward VII is due to attend an event at the British Museum
Underground Station tomorrow. This event marks the king's first
public appearance since his accession, amid growing fears of an
assassination attempt.

The underground station staff are thrilled to be welcoming the king,
along with 100 invited guests, to a special reception on the platform
to mark the king's accession and the recent opening of the British
Museum's own underground station. We, too, here at the *Herald* are
excited to hear the king is returning to royal duties and we are relieved
that our fear for his highness' life has proved ~~unsubstantiated~~.
legitimate

~~LONG LIVE~~ THE KING!
Down with

Our way in

"It's 12!" Watson exclaims.

"Yes, yes, I know, Watson," you retort, as you rush over to display case 12.

Your eyes scan the case and land on a newspaper clipping.

"This must be what they've been planning."

"But we're stuck here. How do we stop them?" Watson sounds worried.

Your finger points to the small sketch. "Watson, my dear fellow," you say slowly, "I think these are tunnels..."

"They remind me of something," you muse. "The map, Watson. Look at the map and find them."

As Watson pores over the map, you make your way back to the centre of the Manuscript Saloon.

▶ *Turn to 49*

"Rather familiar," Watson says, drily, as you re-enter the Archaic Room. "Why have we been sent back here?"

"Perhaps there is something we missed and we need to keep looking..."

Time for another pipe, and some thought. You light up, and the flame of your match throws light on the nearby display case.

"Look over there," you say, pointing with the end of your pipe.

One of the collection items is missing – there is clearly an empty space on the floor.

"I wonder, Holmes, if there's something significant in these moved and missing items?"

"No doubt. They could be clues for us, you mean. Well, what does the card say?"

STRANGFORD APOLLO

Archaic kouros statue, dates to circa 500–490 BC. Marble. Possibly linked to pediments in the Temple of Aphaia at Aegina. More recently, it has been thought to be perhaps from Boetia. God of truth and prophecy, healing, diseases, the Sun, poetry, music, dance and so on.

"Some letters are underlined, I see."

"Eagle-eyed as ever, Watson."

What do they spell out?

▶ *Consult the map – Turn to the number you discover*

You rush out of the Mediaeval Room, down the main staircase and to the Reading Room entrance. The door now stands open. Someone knew you were coming. It feels odd to be almost back where you started. Are you going in circles? Or are you getting somewhere?

As soon as you enter the Reading Room your eyes are drawn upwards. Through the curved windows you can see the first glimmers of daylight. Your heart skips a single beat. Time does rather seem to be running out. In the low light you can just discern something scratched onto one of the glass panels. You narrow your eyes.

"It is rather magnificent, isn't it?" Watson pulls you from your trance.

"See that, Watson?" you point up at the window pane. "There's something there, but I can't seem to quite work out what it is."

Watson shifts his footing and peers through the glasses perched on the end of his nose. "It seems to look like... It's a hieroglyph, Holmes."

You look around and notice a white envelope lying on a far table. You sigh. You have grown to rather detest these little messages. Watson walks over. He opens the letter. It reads:

> *Aha, we meet again! And again and again... I've left you a symbol, Holmes. Or is it two, perhaps? Or three? Or five? How many times do you see me? The number tells you where to go next.*

"Better get counting then, Holmes." Watson turns to you and smiles. You sigh again, and your eyes begin to scan the room.

▶ *Turn to the number you discover*

JEAN-JACQUES O'SULLIVAN

from 47

"It was before your time, Watson. I had just set up shop as a consulting detective in Montague Street. My client list was modest as I applied, even then, that rigorous principle that I hold to now: a case must above all be interesting.

"Montague Street is but a short dash to the British Museum where, I must confess I spent a good deal of time, as it was far warmer and more comfortable than my modest garret.

"I quickly acquired a ticket for the Reading Room – I was researching into the composition of London clays – and soon struck up an acquaintance with a young geologist. I had impressed him on our first meeting by deducing that he was unmarried, had a French mother and an Irish father, and had fought in the Franco-Prussian War. He had, in fact, lost a leg in the conflict and supported himself everywhere using a very fine crutch – a very expensive bespoke Paton & Shields model made entirely of aluminium. Apparently, a gift from his French aunt."

"How the deuce did you know about his mother and father?" I asked, intrigued in spite of myself.

"Elementary," he smirked. "I took the opportunity of glancing at his Reading Room ticket; his name was Jean-Jacques O'Sullivan."

He can be infuriating sometimes.

▶ *Turn to 114*

Held up against a source of light, the note displays a hidden message.

"Hmm," you say. "A silly bird?... Gather our papers?"

"What's this, Holmes?" Watson asks, pointing. "There are some letters in bold type in the document."

"I'll wager the bold letters will give us some clue as to what to do next," you opine confidently.

You set about reading the code.

▶ *If you think you should go to the fireplace – Turn to 19*

▶ *If you think you should go to the desk – Turn to 27*

My esteemed genius Mr Ho**l**mes and his
foolish friend,

    Buona sera. If you're reading this I kn**o**w you
have tumbled headlong into my trap. You are my
pris**o**ners for the night. Genius, did I say? I
caught you pretty easily, like a silly w**e**e bird.
    In any case, what kind of genius would be stuc**k**
for so long over the Conk-Singleton papers I laid
in your path?
    Woul**d** you say you were an anarchist, Mr Holmes?
A hater of authority? A violent man? By the time
this night has ended I predict y**o**u will be seen
in that light by the powers that be. Eve**n** by your
brother. You will be shamed.
    You sent my brilliant friend, my inspiration, to
his death. **T**hat struggle was in a high place. But
t**h**is one will **end** in profondità.I am preparing for
you th**e** lingering death of imprisonment.
    Gather your paper**s**, Sir, and play the game.
By the Gree**k** rocks, count the cards and repeat
your bet. Prepare to go down, even into
underground realms.
    I wish you buona fortuna. You have until
morning. By then you will either be free or
tangled even more deliciously in the trap I have
laid for you.

---- Bonaparte

ESCAPED?

Watson strides to the far end of the Manuscript Saloon and pushes open the door. You walk through, and find yourself once again in the Grenville Library. The six candles have now burnt themselves out. The candle stubs remind you of the man with the gruff voice from earlier that evening.

"Hold hard there, Watson. Something feels a little... odd," you venture. "I felt that man was trying to lead us somewhere, but actually we've just been round in a circle."

Do you go back to the Manuscript Saloon or continue to the front of the Museum?

▶ *Go back to the Manuscript Saloon – Turn to 28*

▶ *Continue to the Front Colonnade – Turn to 103*

ARCHAIC ROOM

You follow the sounds into the Archaic Room. As soon as you enter they subside. You can't see anyone there.

Moonlight falling through a high window hits some of the statues and displays so they glow almost silver, but you can't see any human figures.

"Whoever it was making that noise now seems to have scarpered," Watson murmurs.

Or is he lying low, keeping an eye on us? you think.

Something catches your eye on a series of tomb fragments on the other side of the room. You indicate the direction with your head.

Watson strikes a match and reads the card. "Harpy Tomb, from Xanthos, capital of Lycia."

"What more does it say about them, Watson?"

"Harpies – winged messengers that carry the souls of the dead."

"Like Hermes Psychopompus," you say.

"I always was entranced by his winged sandals," Watson muses. "And Mercury with his winged feet – anatomically intriguing."

"Can we concentrate on the task at hand?" you chide.

"Let us look a little closer at this. There are pieces of mirror balanced against the tomb fragments," you say.

"What could that mean, Holmes? Are we supposed to look at ourselves? Are we 'the dead'?"

"Perhaps they're showing us where to go."

"You mean, behind us?"

"Not quite – a reflection of where we are now."

▶ *Turn to the reflection of this entry*

⑲ AT THE FIREPLACE

from 16

You wander over to the fireplace. The mantle is covered with a thick layer of dust. There is a picture of the museum director with Sir Alisdair, standing in front of the Museum gates. You think of the documents he gave you, and wonder whether perhaps there might be some more to be found in here.

Watson calls you over to the director's desk.

"I say, Holmes, old man – come and see what I've found."

You walk over to join him.

▶ *Turn to 27*

Next, you look at the pattern of the ties on the columns.

"Could it be a number sequence, Holmes, do you think?"

You look at him, witheringly. "Yes, of course it could, dear chap. And what would be the next number in the sequence?"

He scratches his head and groans. You look up to admire the stars and twinkling Venus, while the old boy's brain grinds through its gears. Finally, he shrugs despairingly.

"Yes," you say. "There is no sequence. But could it be a simple sum?"

"Would you add them up or subtract them, d'you think?"

"Those are not the only options, Watson," you say, giving him a long-suffering look. "Division, I grant you, does not work because the sum would break down at divide by zero. But multiplication is as feasible as subtraction or addition."

"I would say you get a more sensible answer if you add the figures up," Watson continues, ignoring you. "And these chalked marks by your feet could be addition signs."

"Then again, should we use the Translation Device?" you wonder. There must be a way of entering this information into the Device.

You both walk swiftly across the forecourt to the front of the Museum. The giant doors are slightly ajar. Inside, it seems deserted.

Where to?

▶ *If you don't think there is a pattern – Turn to 89*

▶ *If you think you should use the Translation Device – Turn to 3*

▶ *If you think it's an addition, multiplication or subtraction sum, work out the answer – Turn to the number you discover*

UNDERGROUND RELIEF?

"It's 21," Watson responds, "The hour, then the minute."

"Hmmm," you muse. You're not entirely convinced.

You follow Watson as he winds around the cabinets to display case 21.

"A clipping," Watson points out.

You look down into the display case below.

"What a relief," Watson sighs. "There can be no plot after all, Holmes. How are they going to assassinate the king if he isn't leaving the palace?"

You say nothing.

"It is a little odd though, isn't it, Holmes?" Watson looks at you. "To have sent us all around the Museum, searching for this plot, only to tell us it isn't going to happen."

"It is in our opponents' style, though," you admit reluctantly. "They seem to like watching me suffer."

"Let's get out of here, then!" Watson beams at you as he takes the map out of his pocket.

You walk back to the centre of the Manuscript Saloon. Something still doesn't seem right.

▶ *Turn to 49*

KING EDWARD VII CANCELS ALL PUBLIC ENGAGEMENTS

King Edward VII announced today that he plans to cancel all public engagements for the foreseeable future. The act is understood to be in response to growing assassination fears. A death threat has been seen scrawled on the outer walls at Buckingham Palace, and who knows how many more are landing with the king inside?

Unfortunately, this act has done little to improve good favour. Many are now scrambling to replace the king as a key speaker or dignified guest.

We at the *Herald* can only hope that soon the king can return to his official duties, but wish him well in the meantime.

LONG LIVE THE KING!

A STRANGE ENCOUNTER

You walk back through the corridors to the King's Library. Suddenly, a figure appears out of the darkness, directly in front of you. You stop dead in your tracks. Is it Moran? Lady Conk-Singleton? It is, in fact, just the disconcertingly handsome cleaner once more. He is heading straight for you. You try to get out of the way, but you don't quite make it, and he gently brushes against you as he moves past.

You think you hear the words, "Good luck. Top left, bottom right," very gently spoken.

"Hello!" you call after him as he recedes into the darkness. "Hello? Who are you? Were you talking to me?" The figure continues walking. You linger for a moment and then rush ahead to meet Watson.

"Top left, bottom right, Watson. Write that down before I forget. I'm not sure what it means yet. It definitely means something!"

You push open the big doors to the King's Library once again.

▶ *Turn to 69*

TOWARDS THE READING ROOM

Watson turns towards the noise and hesitates.

"Come along, Watson," you urge. "To the Reading Room."

Watson trots behind, holding the floor plan.

As you arrive, you see a slender figure, sweeping the floor.

Perhaps you caught a glimpse of this same cleaner earlier? He is propping something up against the door.

The fellow hurries towards you and smiles. He has a strange smudge of a moustache above rather full, red lips.

He really is an uncommonly attractive man, you find yourself thinking.

"Stop!" you say. "What were you doing? Where were you going?"

The cleaner looks at you, smiles and puts a finger to his lips. That look! There's something tantalisingly familiar about it...

▶ *Turn to 87*

(24) CATALOGUE ROOM

The Catalogue Room is crammed full of documents and huge tomes.

"Holmes, there's a puzzle scrawled above this diagram."

You join Watson and look at the book lying open on the desk.

"It's a book of patents," you say. "What's it doing here?"

Watson points at the text below the diagram. "Look, it's a patent for the Singleton Security System."

"Why are they showing us now?"

"Come on, old chap," Watson chides you. "The puzzle!"

▶ *If you'd like to examine the patent for the Singleton Security System –*
Turn to the back of the book, then return here

▶ *Turn to 90*

(25) BANGING AND WHISTLING

Just then, from the direction of the Director's Office, you hear some banging and whistling.

"We need to retrace our steps," you say. "And I think someone is trying to get our attention."

"Isn't that...?" Watson wonders.

"The Internazionale. Yes."

You head towards the noise.

▶ *Turn to 18*

㉖ INSIDE THE DIRECTOR'S OFFICE

from 6

Once inside the Director's Office, you look around. You're not quite sure what you're looking for. You go to pull the map out of your pocket, and the blank piece of paper from the assistant director's jacket falls to the floor.

"No man carries a blank sheet of paper around with him, wouldn't you say, Watson?"

You notice a candle burning at the other end of the room.

"How odd," Watson says, "I would have thought they would blow out the candles when closing up?"

▶ *You hold the blank piece of paper up to the flame – Turn to 16*

▶ *You sit down to smoke a pipe – Turn to 104*

㉗ AN INVITATION

from 16, 19

Watson points at the invitation lying on the director's desk.

"M. Napoleon, it says here, Holmes... and the blighter who wrote the hidden message signed himself Bonaparte. Didn't you call your Professor Moriarty 'The Napoleon of Crime'?"

"Absolutely, Watson. But, as you know, Moriarty is dead. He fell to his death from the Reichenbach Falls."

"But this cad... this fellow speaks of sending 'my brilliant friend, my inspiration, to his death.'"

Not uninteresting, you think.

▶ *Turn to 2*

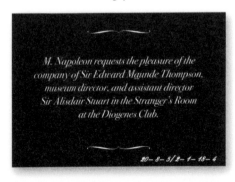

M. Napoleon requests the pleasure of the company of Sir Edward Maunde Thompson, museum director, and assistant director Sir Alisdair Stuart in the Stranger's Room at the Diogenes Club.

20– 8– 5/ 2– 1– 18– 4

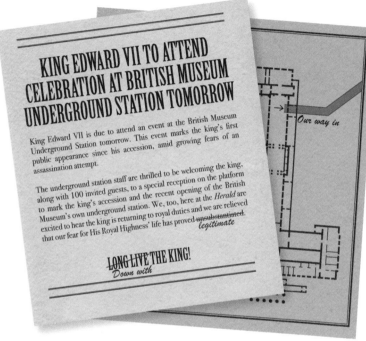

KING EDWARD VII TO ATTEND
CELEBRATION AT BRITISH MUSEUM
UNDERGROUND STATION TOMORROW

King Edward VII is due to attend an event at the British Museum
Underground Station tomorrow. This event marks the king's first
public appearance since his accession, amid growing fears of an
assassination attempt.

The underground station staff are thrilled to be welcoming the king,
along with 100 invited guests, to a special reception on the platform
to mark the king's accession and the recent opening of the British
Museum's own underground station. We, too, here at the *Herald* are
excited to hear the king is returning to royal duties and we are relieved
that our fear for His Royal Highness' life has proved ~~unsubstantiated~~
legitimate

~~LONG LIVE THE KING!~~
Down with

Our way in →

You follow Watson back into the Manuscript Saloon.

It's almost daylight outside. You really are nearly out of time.

"See here, Holmes," Watson beckons you over. "This article is about
the king," he says, tapping at the glass. "This must be where they plan to
shoot him."

"Watson, my dear fellow. These definitely look like underground tunnels
to me."

Watson is already pulling the map out of his pocket.

"They match the drawing in the King's Library," Watson says, heading
for the door.

You follow him.

▶ *Turn to 22*

㉙ ARCHAEOLOGIST MISSING AT SEA

DISAPPEARANCE OF BELLA RABIA

MISSING ITALIAN ARCHAEOLOGIST 'BRILLIANT BUT CONTROVERSIAL' BELLA RABIA LOST AT SEA? STORM IN AEGEAN – THREE SHIPS LOST

31 October 1899

Italian archaeologist Bella Rabia – notorious for her support of anarchist causes and her connection to the late criminal mastermind Professor Moriarty – has disappeared while returning from a visit to the new archaeological digs at Knossos on the island of Crete. Signora Rabia – perhaps the world's only working female archaeologist and one of the most brilliant women of her generation – is known for her outspoken attacks on the very institution of kingship. She was a little-known associate of Professor Moriarty, who died at the Reichenbach Falls, Switzerland, in 1893. This year she had been working on the excavation of Villa Boscoreale near Pompeii, but took a break to visit feted British archaeologist Sir Arthur Evans at his new dig on the island of Crete. Tragedy apparently struck in the form of a major storm on the 'wine-dark sea' of the Aegean.

▶ *Examine the other documents – Turn to 110*

(30) OTHERWISE OCCUPIED

You refuse to go.

"I'm afraid I'm rather busy," you say, turning away brusquely.

Watson goes so far as to touch you on the arm.

"Holmes, I say, bad form, old man. I am rather shocked."

"Well, Watson, you don't achieve excellence by being easily distracted."

You turn away from Watson to find a burly attendant with a big beard standing in front of you. He peers at you through a pair of tiny gold spectacles.

"Mr Holmes, please would ye come this way? The assistant director seems to be doomed. It is a matter of life and death."

"Scottish, are you, my good sir?" Watson says. "Where are you from?"

The attendant merely smiles.

Watson looks at you, and then at the attendant. You can see his doctor's brain at work, trying to measure the man, to seek out the facts in the situation. The burly attendant seemed to say the word 'doomed' with relish. And his Scottish accent is not quite convincing.

You make a mental note to return here later as you follow the man to the Trustees' Room. He did say it was a matter of life and death, after all.

▶ *Go to the Trustees' Room – Turn to 71*

RUMPUS AT SOCIETY WEDDING

SOCIETY WEDDING OF 1900
SIR CRISPIN CONK-SINGLETON TO WED MYSTERIOUS ITALIAN BRIDE
CEREMONY IN WESTMINSTER ABBEY ON 28 SEPTEMBER
RECEPTION AFTERWARDS IN ST JAMES'S SQUARE MANSION

6 May 1900

Sir Crispin Conk-Singleton is to wed a mysterious Italian beauty known only as 'the Lady Arabella'. Little is known of the bride, who was first seen in the society pages covering this summer's events – though she has been seen frequently at the British Museum examining their archaeological artefacts. Sir Crispin, heir to a vast fortune and several large estates, has recently shocked society by founded a lock-making firm, which recently released the Singleton Security System.

▶ *Examine the other documents – Turn to 110*

BOOKSHELVES

Watson wanders away from you, map in hand. He is so absorbed in it that he almost walks into three separate bookcases.

"Watson! For goodness sake, dear fellow!" you shout after him. "Look where you are going! And hurry up!"

Watson turns, looking confused.

"Holmes, there is a 32 on the map, and it appears that the room we're looking for is just here." Watson points at a bookshelf directly in front of him, and looks at you quizzically.

You say nothing. You wait for it to fall into place.

"I don't understand. This is a bookshelf. How do I...?"

Watson reaches out to the bookshelf in frustration. The bookcase moves under the pressure of his hand.

"Good Lord!" The look of surprise on Watson's face is worth it.

The bookcase opens up like a door to reveal a small, winding staircase.

"Well, up we go then, Watson!" You smile at him.

"How did you know, Holmes? Why didn't you say anything?"

You just smile as Watson heads up the narrow stairs.

▶ *Turn to 43*

TRIANGULATION

from 63, 67

You walk into the Phigaleian Room. Ahead of you, Watson lets out a low whistle. On the floor is a nest of triangles:

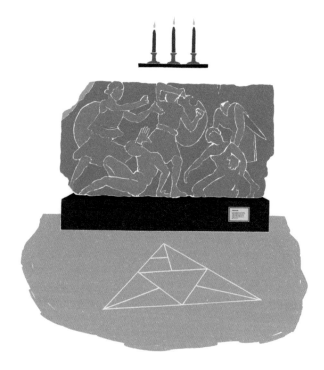

"Watson, can you do the honours?"

Watson squints at the item card. He looks confused. "Holmes, this has all been written over."

"Just read it, old man!" Your temper is running short.

Watson sighs. "It says, Phigaleian Freeze. Then someone's written: Three locked in conflict. So many triples, Mr Holmes. My cunning, your intelligence and Watson's eagerness. My freedom, your self-imprisonment and the king's death. Here we have another dead end, Mr Holmes. Can you triangulate your way back onto the path? Count the triangles. Then multiply by three – for all our triples – to find your way."

You set to work counting the triangles drawn on the floor.

► *Turn to the number you discover*

(34) # MUSIC ROOM

from 73, 82

You walk into the Music Room and gasp. It takes a moment for you to understand what you are seeing. The doors to each display case lie open and instruments are strewn across the floor. A violin lies at your feet. But the strings from all the instruments have been tied up around the room, tracking a route from where you are standing to a door at the other end.

"Such destruction." Watson shakes his head and tuts.

You can't take your eyes off the web of strings. You imagine what it would be like to take your bow to the puzzle, to play these strings across the room.

"It's also a thing of beauty, Watson."

"They seem to lead to images," Watson points. He is right.

Your eyes follow the string at your feet up to a small sketch of a cat. This is connected to an image of an apple, then this to the image of a tree, then to another apple, then a lemon, an orange, a pair of gates, an umbrella, and, finally, to an eye.

"Something to do with letters, perhaps?" Watson turns to you.

"Hmmm, yes," you respond. You are already scribbling.

► *Solve the code, then consult the map –*
Turn to the number you discover

THE ADVENTURE OF THE BRITISH MUSEUM

You head towards the Egyptian Central Saloon.

"This must have been what the letter meant, Watson."

"Central Egypt... Look for the Stone."

The Stone stands tall in front of you. It's mesmerising.

"It was found by Napoleon Bonaparte's men, of course," you say.

"The writing is the same message but written in three different languages – Ancient Greek, hieroglyphic and Demotic – which made it possible to translate the hieroglyphs."

There are additional symbols scratched along the top of the Stone. You put these into the Translation Device. Write the letters in the boxes below.

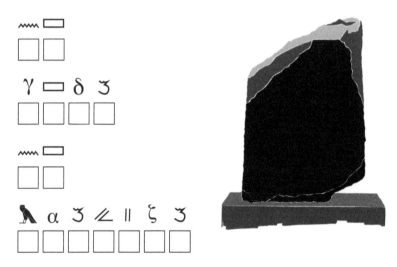

"Any clues on the label, Watson?"

"Yes! 1ROS.YU9 Rosetta Stone. And the text reads: Take first from last and find the room with that number."

▶ *Turn to the number you discover*

You arrive in the Nereid Room and look around. It seems completely dark. The moon must be covered by clouds once more. There is a curious odour... A candle burning?

As you look around for a lead, or instructions, you hear the sound of water being poured.

"What on earth?" Watson exclaims.

"A match please, dear fellow."

The flame flares. You see a series of headless statues on one side of the room. And before them, on the gallery floor, a beautiful Chinese ceramic bowl and a jug filled with water. Someone must have been pouring it. Did you sense a movement in the darkness before the match was struck? A mop stands propped against the far wall.

Watson reads another card: "NER.1RE Nereids. From the tomb of Erbinna in Xanthos."

"What more does it say about them?"

"Sea nymphs, Holmes. Thought to be personifications of the waves. One of them was the consort of sea god Poseidon. There's this IAN here again, too."

He takes a note of the Nereid item code. Then he says, "It goes on: Where to next, Mr Holmes? Are your ideas stagnating? Is your thinking coming in waves? Should you go with the flow?"

You try to focus on what Watson is saying. He yawns. Wretched man. You follow suit.

Suddenly, in the dark gallery you both seem to be overcome with weariness. There are a few chairs conveniently positioned nearby.

"I'm just going to take a moment, Holmes."

▶ *Turn to 101*

LADY ARABELLA'S MATHS CHALLENGE

"Look, Holmes," Watson says, pointing to the back of the letter. "There's something here, too."

You turn the letter over to reveal a small square, which is four columns by four rows and has some numbers inside.

"Aha," Watson smiles. "It's one of those magic squares. Each row, column and diagonal must add up to the same number. Each box contains a number from 1 to 16, and each number can only appear once."

"That box in the bottom row is circled," you muse, tapping it gently with your finger. "Maybe that is some clue as to where we should go next."

You pull out your pencil and set about solving the magic square.

8		14	1
13	2		12
3		9	
	5	(○)	15

▶ *Solve the magic square – Turn to the circled number*

▶ *If you're unsure of the answer – Turn to 105*

㊳ HAND'S ON... THE HANDLE

The rough dirt of the tunnel gives way to a hard floor and you breathe a sigh of relief.

Watson turns to you, excited. "We've made it, Holmes. We're here."

"Let us calm ourselves, Watson," you respond. "We're not quite there yet."

You look around inquisitively. This is pointless. In the pitch black you can barely see your hand in front of your nose. Watson stumbles sideways and bumps into you.

"Oh, Holmes, I'm sorry. Confound it. I just can't seem to find my bearings here." Watson stumbles off, but he has given you an idea.

You close your eyes and track back to the King's Library in your mind, and you run through the calculations... Facing north east, down ten yards, a 45-degree turn clockwise, and six minutes' walking at a pace of three-and-one-tenth miles per hour in a southerly direction should mean the platform is... You turn sharply to your left, reach out, and yes, there is a door.

"Here we go," you say.

You reach down. Your hand fumbles a little at the handle, which feels large and surprisingly heavy. It turns a little too easily.

Then, quite without warning, the handle falls through the door and into the room on the other side. Light spills through the hole and Watson gives the door a gentle kick. It swings open in front of you, revealing a small room, with a gas lamp burning in the far corner.

You step inside.

▶ *Turn to 102*

KING'S LIBRARY

You follow Watson through the doors into the King's Library.

He breaks the silence: "It's a marvellous room to explore, even to be locked in, isn't it, old man?" He looks up at the ceiling high above and the balcony along the walls.

"Quite a length. Almost long enough for a hundred-yard dash," he muses.

"Exactly long enough," you counter. "It is precisely 100 yards in length. I have calculated it from having walked this short section and knowing my own stride. We haven't got time though, Watson. We need to focus."

"I say, Holmes, look at this." He is holding up an envelope addressed to Messenger Watson.

"Where did you find that, Watson?" you say.

"On the table... Messenger, indeed. What can that mean?"

Watson opens the envelope and finds this message:

> *Messenger Watson. Where do the gods live? Some come flying down below, others keep their secrets up on high. Count Holmes. Follow these deliverers to your next prison.*

"Some letters are in red and some are bold," he says.

"Clearly a code," you say.

"Anagrams, perhaps?" Watson murmurs.

"Flying down below," you ponder, "but then up on high."

"What do we know about how the gods send messages, Holmes?" he murmurs.

You are silent, pondering.

▶ *Turn to the number you discover*

▶ *You're not sure what the message is asking you to do. You notice a small door at the end of the library, standing slightly ajar. You head towards it – Turn to 42*

from 45, 85

(40) THE KING'S HEAD

More mischief here. There are scrape marks on the floor.

"Looks as if the head and arm have been moved," Watson says. "And look here on the floor."

You see that a compass has been chalked on the floor.

"See here, Holmes, item AME.9HBN - it's the head and arm of the great Amenhotep III. Great heavens, the head must be at least ten feet tall, old chap!"

You're too busy looking at the chalk markings.

"Maybe he's trying to show us which way to go next," you muse.

"Which direction is the head facing, Holmes?" Watson asks.

You decide to make a note of the appropriate directional letters and enter them into the Translation Device.

▶ *Put the two digits together – Turn to the number you discover*

(41) A WORD FROM WATSON

from 51

You pull Watson into the shadows of the forecourt.

The doctor shouts back from the gateway: "For goodness sake, Mr Holmes, you're causing us additional trouble here – some time we don't have. We have to make haste for the hospital. Goodbye and good luck!"

You look up into the night sky, pondering. You note the doctor's slightly unusual use of the word 'additional'. You glance over towards the front of the Museum – is that the attendant lurking near the door?

But you look away because Watson is now at your elbow, pointing. "Look, Holmes," he sounds excited. "You can see Venus in the sky tonight, named after the Roman goddess of love and beauty. She is rather beautiful, isn't she?"

You barely hear him. Your mind is back in the Museum, turning the case over and over.

▶ *Turn to 9*

LOCKED IN

Ignoring Watson's protests, you push through the door in front of you, with your devoted Boswell following reluctantly.

"Watson!" you shout, just as the door swings shut.

Too late you realize there is a lock on the door. You hear it being turned. You are locked in. Someone outside lets out a high-pitched laugh. You look around slowly. It seems to be a storage room of sorts. Piles of cloth and metal buckets surround you. Not a clue in sight.

You pace up and down, trying to find some exit. Nothing.

Through a small window in a high corner you watch the light change from dark blue, to pink, to pale yellow. Finally, you hear footsteps outside, then a key in the lock. The door swings open.

"Dear Sherlock."

How perfectly dreadful. It is Mycroft. He gives you a superior smile.

"Is the king dead?" Watson groans.

"Fear not," Mycroft says and gives a bark of laughter. "I have rounded up the culprits and saved His Royal Highness."

"Oh, thank goodness." Watson, of course, is pleased.

"Looks like you've got yourself mixed up in some rather unfortunate business," Mycroft says with a notable hint of glee.

You open your mouth to speak.

"No need for that now," Mycroft says quickly. "Your good friend Lestrade is expecting you at the police station."

Mycroft brandishes some handcuffs.

"Goodness, Mycroft, do we really...?"

"You tell me, Sherlock," he says as he snaps the handcuffs around your wrists. "A poisoned assistant director, a forged Rosetta Stone..."

As you approach the Museum entrance, Mycroft says, "Lots of people outside. Let's hope the image of you in handcuffs doesn't stay with them for too long. I suspect a knighthood may be on the cards. I'll invite you to witness the wonderful event, Sherlock."

He hands you a copy of the morning paper and says, "Thank goodness one Holmes was on hand to foil the assassination plot."

THE END

The Daily Gazette

KING EDWARD VII SAVED BY MYCROFT HOLMES

Anarchist Plot to Kill King in British Museum Underground Foiled

LORD AND LADY OF THE REALM IN HANDCUFFS

Sherlock Holmes Humiliated As Leading Government Figure, Brother of the Master Detective, Saves the Day

Is this Sherlock Holmes's greatest humiliation? The Baker Street maestro failed to stop a daring plot to assassinate King Edward VII at an official event in the British Museum Underground Station this morning. The king was saved by leading government figure Mycroft Holmes, the detective's older and seemingly more gifted brother. Lady Arabella Conk-Singleton – now unmasked as missing Italian anarchist Bella Rabia – was arrested at the site with her husband, Lord Crispin Conk-Singleton and British Museum assistant director Sir Alisdair Stuart. Colonel Sebastian Moran, one-time associate of the late Professor Moriarty, was captured red-handed as he prepared his weapon, and taken into custody.

Anarchism Infects High Society

As she was taken away, Lady Arabella said: "It should be taken into account that I gave the great Sherlock Holmes many opportunities to prevent this happening. Despite a host of clues laid by myself and my associates, Sherlock failed to stop the plot. Only Mycroft's superior mind was equal to stopping us."

ROSETTA STONE A FORGERY

The Rosetta Stone on display in the British Museum is a fake. Anarchist plotters hired a skilled stonemason to create a replica and carried off the original, planning to sell it to a wealthy Texan. The original stone has been found in London Docks. The Stone, inscribed in three languages, is a key artefact used to decipher Ancient Egyptian hieroglyphs and was found in Egypt in 1799.

WHISTLE WHILE YOU WORK

from 32

You hurry ahead of Watson and into the Curator's Office. Books are piled high and notes are scattered across the desk. You sigh heavily. You're growing more concerned you won't be able to make it out in time.

"Look at this," calls Watson, a page of musical manuscript in his hand.

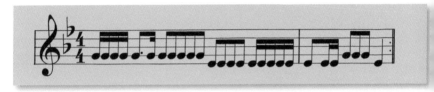

You're well known for your skill on the violin, but even you would struggle to make a tune out of these notes. So many of them are repeated. As he holds up the music, you see the words, 'Go to...' scrawled across the top, and an 'S' scribbled beneath the first set of notes.

"D'you think it's a musical code, Holmes?"

"Certainly... Now, which part of the Museum do the notes lead us to?"

"I know you read music, Holmes," says Watson eagerly, "but I don't believe these notes correspond to letters in the normal way. The first three notes together on the third line are normally 'G', are they not? But the code-writer has indicated the letter 'S'."

"Thank you, Watson, I had noticed that some time ago..."

You perch on the edge of the desk and attempt to break the code.

| S | | | | | | |

▶ *Solve the code – Turn to the number you discover*

▶ *You can't solve the code. You look around the room for more clues and notice a door standing ajar in front of you. You move towards it. Watson follows you, saying, "Hold on, Holmes, don't be hasty..." – Turn to 42*

GOING UNDERGROUND

Watson lifts up the grate. He sticks his head through the hole.

"By Jove, you are right, old man!" he exclaims. His voice reverberates. "There seems to be some sort of tunnel down here."

You glance around the room one final time and spot a solitary candle burning in a far corner. You pick it up before joining Watson, who has now lowered himself into the underground tunnel. The tunnel is dirty and small and extends to your left and right, directly east and west. You hold the candle up and peer down the paths. They seem identical.

"Which way?" you wonder aloud.

"Here, Holmes, come and look." Watson beckons you over. He points to a message carved into the dirt.

"It's that damn code again!" Watson sighs. "If people are going to use these ancient languages I do wish they would at least do it properly."

Which way do you go?

▶ *If you think you should go east – Turn to 74*

▶ *If you think you should go west – Turn to 96*

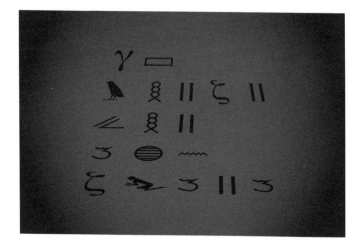

(45) RIGHT YOU ARE... OR ARE YOU?

from 8

You turn right, heading to the Southern Egyptian Gallery.

Watson touches your arm. "Are you sure, Holmes? Wouldn't you say the word 'sinister' was a clue? Indicating that we should go left?"

You head back and turn left.

▶ *Turn to 40*

(46) A SMUGGLED MAP

from 109

"O'Sullivan looked at it and whistled in amazement. It meant nothing to me. 'Sacré bleu, Holmes,' he breathed, excitedly. 'This is Paradol's legendary map of the bauxite deposits in the Jajce region of Bosnia-Herzogovina. It was thought lost. It is unique. Whoever has this can get early access to a huge source of the ore needed to make aluminium, and corner the market. In the wrong hands... well.'

"We returned to the Museum, where we met an ashen-faced librarian on the steps. 'Mr Holmes,' he cried. 'I need your help.' He knew of my skills as I had done a little discreet academic thief-finding for him. He went on: 'I fear we have lost a very valuable map,' just as I handed him the red cylinder and said, 'Do not agitate yourself, Sir; I believe this is the map you are looking for?'

"As he gaped in incredulity, I explained: 'I suspect that it was the work of the Brotherhood of the Red Hand, a Balkan anarchist group wanting to raise funds for their cause. They smuggled the map out in Mr O'Sullivan's crutch so as not to arouse suspicion. You must keep it better locked up.'

"Leaving the librarian agape, O'Sullivan and I strolled away. The crutch thief turned out to be a wanted man, the leader of an anarchist cell that Scotland Yard had been trying to crack for some time.

"A feather in the cap for the young policeman who nabbed him, eh, Watson... One Constable G. Lestrade!" Holmes laughed, delightedly.

And with that he went back to his handstands, whistling 'Ode to Joy'.

THE END

THE AFFAIR OF THE ALUMINIUM CRUTCH

"Tcha!"

I hurled my newspaper across the breakfast table. I'll admit I was not in the best of moods. Incessant rain lashed against the windows. My leg hurt damnably, as it always did in wet weather. And my tea was cold.

"You fume, Watson, you fret," said Sherlock, who was practising handstands against the mantelpiece – a new hobby for him: he claimed that the rush of blood to his head refreshed his brain.

I glared at him. We had no cases on, yet there he was, chipper as a terrier with two tails, standing on his head, and merrily humming snatches from light opera.

My eyes darted suspiciously to the silver casket where he kept his paraphernalia, but I was not quick enough.

"Ah, Watson," he twinkled merrily, springing lightly to the upright, "you wrong me; this is sheer joie de vivre, I have had no recourse to any solution. What has put you out of countenance?"

"Confound it, Holmes," I snarled. "Mrs Hudson has been playing fast and loose with the egg timer, again; my shares in the Acme Aluminum Company have taken a battering; and my leg hurts. Why are you so bally cheerful?"

"Allow me to lead you out of your Stygian dumps," he trilled.

I indicated somewhat mulishly that I thought this unlikely.

Holmes was unperturbed, and began packing his pipe with that vile black shag he favours.

"Aluminium," he mused, bouncing up and down on the balls of his feet and sucking at the briar. "A wonderful metal – light, strong, modern, malleable, impervious to rust. I recall, my dear Watson, an early case of mine involving aluminium. A light affair, but entertaining. You might care to write it up – the exercise might put you in a better temper."

He was positively beaming.

I almost threw my egg spoon at him.

▶ *Turn to 15*

A TICKET TO READ

"What do you make of all this?" Watson murmurs.

You are silent.

You pick up the Reading Room ticket. "Remarkable," you breathe.

"What's that?"

"Well, you'll know, Watson, that you have to apply in writing to the principal librarian for access to the Reading Room and you receive a personalized card."

"Yes, old chap."

"Well, this ticket is made out in my name. Someone has applied in my name. It reads: Mr Sherlock Holmes – for researches into the Conk-Singleton Case."

"They seem to have everything about you jotted down, old chum," Watson says. "And look here. There are some curious symbols scribbled."

More and more extraordinary.

▶ *Turn to 86*

CHOICE OF TWO LIBRARIES

A shiver threads itself up your spine. You love these moments when everything begins to fall into place. You are very keen to get on.

"Where to then, Watson?" you demand.

"Well," Watson retorts, "your guess is as good as mine, Holmes. Either we go on towards the front entrance through the Grenville Library, or we go back to the King's Library."

"It's a choice of two libraries," you mutter to yourself.

"But which is it, Holmes?" Watson responds testily. "Forwards to the Grenville Library, or back to the King's?"

▶ *Head to the Grenville Library – Turn to 17*

▶ *Head to the King's Library – Turn to 22*

TRIUMPH

from 70

Watson gently moves the dials to their positions and turns the knobs left and right. He takes a deep breath and pushes. The door swings open.

Watson turns to you. "We've done it, Holmes. We've foiled them!"

You allow a smile to tickle at your lips.

"Yes, Watson, this time I think we have."

You pick up the gun from the floor and the gas lamp from the far wall, and follow Watson back through the tunnels and up into the King's Library. The room is lit with a golden hue. Sunlight streams through the windows.

"Holmes! Watson!" a familiar voice calls. You turn. It's Mycroft.

"We heard that you'd been trapped here, Holmes." Mycroft pats your shoulder in a manner that is honestly a little condescending. "Don't worry, we're here to help you."

You smile back and hand Mycroft the Mannlicher, still heavy in your hands. He looks at you, confused.

"There is going to be an attempted regicide," you say. "Today, at the British Museum Underground Station. You'll be able to find the anarchists on the train tracks at 9 a.m." Mycroft looks stunned.

"Come on then, Mycroft," you say, smiling. "Get on after them, do your job."

Mycroft looks at you, and then, as though he has been shocked, he starts moving very quickly towards the door.

"The Rosetta Stone is a fake!" you shout after him as he walks away.

Mycroft splutters. "What?!" he shouts, before turning and running towards the Museum entrance.

You turn and smile at Watson. He claps you on the back and grins. You head for home.

▶ *Turn to 65*

from 115

(51) OUTSIDE THE MUSEUM

You hear a scraping sound and look up.

The doctor and two attendants have lifted the assistant director onto a stretcher and are starting to leave. Something falls out of the assistant director's hand, landing gently on the floor. You see Watson bend quickly to pocket it.

"Come along, Mr Holmes, Dr Watson," the doctor says.

The Museum is now closed; staff are hurrying you out of the door.

Outside, twilight is settling over London but it is still just light enough to see. You all hurry across the forecourt in front of the Museum. The two attendants carry the assistant director out through the main gates, with the doctor scurrying behind them.

You're frustrated that you didn't make more progress with the hieroglyphs and Greek letters, and the fascinating Conk-Singleton Case.

"Come along, please!" one of the attendants shouts impatiently.

Do you follow or do you try to go back into the Museum?

▶ *Follow the attendant – Turn to 72*

▶ *Try to go back into the Museum – Turn to 41*

(52) ARE YOU SURE?

from 7

Watson examines the map.

"I can't see 52 on the map, Holmes. Are you sure that's the right answer?"

"Hmmm."

"Have you had a look at the Reading Room ticket?" Watson asks. "That had some similar symbols on it. Maybe that's the first part of the sequence."

▶ *Look at the sequence – Turn to 7*

▶ *Head towards Room 52 – Turn to 42*

DEAD END?

"THE DEAD?"

"There are of course plenty of connections to the dead in a place like this Museum."

"I couldn't make sense of that code, Watson, for our purposes."

"It feels like he's taunting us."

"Or she, Watson?" You are wondering about Lady Conk-Singleton and whether she might be connected to the plot.

Watson ignores you. Not for the first time.

"Hmmm."

Watson is holding the invitation up in front of him.

"Aha, I have it. It is to do with Shakespeare," you say.

"How on Earth?"

"Look on the back of the invitation."

He turns it over. "It says 2B/2B."

"Clear enough, even for you, old man?"

"Eh?"

You roll your eyes. "To Be or Not to Be? The Prince of Denmark?"

Your eyes scan the room, and land on the bookcase. *The Collected Works of Shakespeare* is sticking out slightly.

You walk over and lift the book off the shelf. It opens in your hand.

It's actually not a book at all, but some sort of secret storage.

Inside, you find two things...

► *A blank map of the Museum layout – Turn to 106*

► *A ticket for the Reading Room – Turn to 107*

(54) A HELPFUL CLEANER

from 87

The cleaner is still lingering.

"Still here, Mr Holmes?" The cleaner says in a high voice. "Sometimes letter codes like this work by displacement. So instead of the whole alphabet being moved around, you just need to know how many places it has shifted. So here 'A' has become 'Z', 'B' has become 'A', and so on..."

Again, you have a maddening sense that you know this person, or that he looks rather like someone you know.

"Try again with the code."

Over in one of the rooms nearby you hear banging and a whistled tune.

After a little while, when you are still scratching your head over the code, the cleaner says, "What's that noise? Don't you want to go and investigate?"

"Isn't that...?" Watson wonders.

"The Internazionale. Yes."

You head towards the noise. Watson is behind you.

► Turn to 18

(55) TROUBLE WITH ROOM NUMBERS

from 99

"I don't know what you're talking about," Watson says. "I see a Room 0, but there is no Room 3, or 1, or 31, or 310..."

"Alright, alright," you snap. "No Room 3102, either. I'm sure the map is a part of the solution, though."

"But take a look at the letter, Holmes. What do you see there?"

"Ah – 3 in column one, 1 in column two, and so on."

"I would say that the pattern on the front of the Museum deliberately echoes the arrangement of the hieroglyphs and letters in the message," Watson says sagely. "There's intelligence at work. I'm not usually the one to say this sort of thing, I know, but there is always a first time. Holmes, we have to try to get back into the locked Museum."

For once, you're grateful to him.

► Turn to 62

CONCENTRATE ON THE DETAILS

from 11

"I have the impression we're involved in a dirty plot," Watson says.

"We should not trust general impressions, but concentrate on the details. What do we know so far, Watson?"

"Number one: The assistant director, Sir Alisdair, was trying very hard to get you here. Number two: In the end you received a letter from Lady Conk-Singleton."

"Not someone we know well, although there is a connection to my rather trying brother and his tiresome gentlemen's club."

"In her letter we learnt that, number three: We were looking for a Stone in the middle of Egypt. And four: The king is in danger and will go underground."

"There was a note that forgery is afoot," you say.

"We know that coded messages have been left around the Museum and Sir Alisdair was in possession of a Device that helps decipher them. He also had news clippings about the Conk-Singleton wedding and the mysterious and beautiful Bella Rabia, the archaeologist with anarchist sympathies."

"The Museum attendant," Watson goes on, "who seems to be none other than the very dangerous Colonel Moran in disguise, was strangely keen for us to remain in the Museum, or return to it once we had left."

"I have also encountered a museum cleaner whose presence here tonight, when the Museum is closed, is difficult to explain," you offer.

"Some items have clearly been moved. I'm noting their item codes," Watson says, tapping his notebook with his pen.

"There is a connection to anarchism and to someone who speaks Italian."

"And a plot that endangers a king," he says. "We have until morning to prevent it."

"We've been told to follow the noise…" Your mind begins to wander.

"And now this piece of classical sculpture has been manhandled to send us another message about royal assassination and anarchist plotters."

You stop listening and look around for fresh information.

▶ *Turn to 68*

(57) LOOK FOR MORE CLUES

from 0

You don't think there's a message.

"Look here, don't give up, my dear fellow. Our careful puzzling led us here. Let's stay and look for more clues."

You hear a rattling of keys over by the main Museum entrance. You walk quickly out of the Grenville Library in time to see the attendant swing the great door shut, lock it and put away the keys.

"What was that?" Watson asks.

"We're locked in." You feel a sense of excitement rather than doom.

After a few moments you hear a soft chuckle.

"Mr Holmes, Dr Watson. What are ye doing here? Enjoying some scriptural studies? Come along, please, I have something to show ye. Ye are slower than I expected tonight."

The attendant takes you towards Room 6.

▶ *Turn to 75*

(58) A TERRIBLE ACT

from 68

You decode it. "The plan is to kill our very own king. It says: Edward VII is dead."

"We must stop this terrible thing from happening. It is awful."

"On the contrary, Watson, it is rather delicious."

"Delicious? What the devil do you mean, Holmes?"

"What time is it, Watson?"

"Don't you have your watch?"

"It's on the operating table at Baker Street. It stopped this morning. I was working on its innards when the letter came and we hurried over here."

"Well, I can't help you. Mine stopped after it got wet in the rain on the way here. I would guess it's 9 or 10 p.m. by now."

▶ *Turn to 63*

(59) A SMALL MISTAKE

You peer closer at the Translation Device and tap it. One of the letters has slipped!

▶ *Try again – Turn to 115*

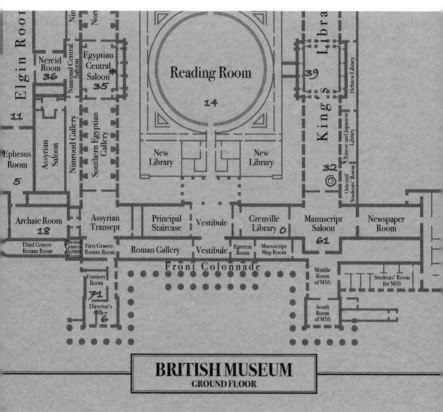

HUMILIATION

Watson gently moves the dials to their positions and turns the knobs to the left and right. He takes a deep breath and pushes. The door doesn't budge. He pushes harder, but nothing moves. You sigh.

"I was so sure," Watson says, absent-mindedly stroking his beard.

You sink to the floor. You wait. It gets closer and closer to the king's planned visit at 9 a.m. You imagine the days ahead, sat in a cell like this one.

There is a scuffle behind you and you turn.

"She-e-e-r-lock," someone calls in a sing-song voice.

Mycroft is standing on the platform looking over at you. He looks far too happy.

"What are you doing there, Sherlock?" he calls. "And with a gun? You weren't...?" He puts a hand to his chest in mock horror. "You weren't going to assassinate the king, were you?"

You breathe a sigh. It is a combination of relief and disdain. "Will you just come and get me out of here, please?"

Mycroft smiles. "Someone is on their way now." He wanders across the platform. "We prevented the regicide, but unfortunately the conspirators got away."

You stand up and brush the dirt off your clothes.

"Oh, and we've discovered the Rosetta Stone is a forgery!" Mycroft shouts over to you. You can hear the glee in his voice. "I hope you played no part in that, Sherlock. But let's take you down to the police station all the same, shall we?"

Your blood begins to boil.

Watson gives you a look as if to say 'this shall soon pass'. Watson always was a good chap.

"Let's hope we don't see the king on the way out, Holmes," Mycroft squeals. "What an embarrassment that would be!"

You lean against the wall and wait for someone to come and open the door.

You are safe, but it'll take years for you to live this down.

Mycroft shows you the morning paper.

THE END

The Daily Gazette

KING EDWARD VII SAVED BY MYCROFT HOLMES
Anarchist Plot to Kill King in British Museum Underground Foiled
SHERLOCK HOLMES HUMILIATED

Moran, one-time associate of the late Professor Moriarty, was seen near the location but ran off into the crowds. Lady Arabella Conk-Singleton praised Mycroft Holmes: "Thank goodness this brave man was on hand to prevent this atrocity happening. It would have been a terrible occurrence and we would have hoisted a black flag had it occurred." Mrs Irene Norton said: "I am most disappointed in Sherlock." When asked why, she only said: "He seems to have lost his touch." She would not comment further. American-born Mrs Norton, née Adler, is a former opera singer who had an impressive career as a contralto, performing at La Scala, Milan, and in the Imperial Opera, Warsaw. She also reputedly trained as an actress and has had a long association with Mr Holmes since their involvement in the affair reported by Dr John Watson as 'A Scandal in Bohemia' ten years ago. Mr Holmes was a witness at Miss Adler's marriage to English lawyer Godfrey Norton.

Is this Sherlock Holmes's greatest humiliation? The Baker Street maestro failed to stop a daring plot to assassinate King Edward VII at an official event in the British Museum Underground Station this morning. The king was prevented from attending the event by leading government figure Mycroft Holmes, the detective's older and seemingly more gifted brother, who is surely now due a knighthood.

Anarchists Escape Capture

The plotters – believed to be the notorious Bonapartist anarchist group – have all escaped to fight another day. Colonel Sebastian

THE AFFAIR OF THE ALUMINIUM CRUTCH

Turn to page 47 to read more about the sensational discovery of a legendary map thought lost forever, and the arrest of its thief, who is now believed to be leader of a rival anarchist group, the Brotherhood of the Red Hand.

You follow Watson back down the staircase and into the Manuscript Saloon. After the grandeur of the King's Library this feels decidedly plain. Your eyes scan the cabinets, full of yellowing documents. Out of the corner of your eye you see a glint of white. You look closer.

Watson follows your eye. "It's an envelope," he says. "A letter."

Watson trots off across the room to collect it. The room is silent apart from the sound of your breath, Watson's footsteps and the ticking of the clock on the wall. Tick – tock – tick. Finally, a clock. You look up eagerly. You can feel the time pressure weighing on you. Each tick of the clock feels like an attack.

"Holmes, it is addressed to you."

With every passing year, we grow older, Holmes. Minutes pass by, we sit and watch the clocks. Hour by hour they tick, we are almost at our future.

You turn the words over in your mind, wondering.

"She's trying to direct us to one of these display cases. But which one?" you muse aloud. Each thought is punctuated by a tick – tock.

"We don't have time to look through them all, Holmes!" Watson sounds concerned.

The clock! You look up. Something isn't right. The time doesn't correspond to the light outside the window. You look down. A pocket watch lies on the table in front of you.

"The clock, Watson!" you cry. "It's wrong."

"Maybe that's our clue, Holmes," Watson responds eagerly. "Perhaps the clock can tell us which display case to look in."

You look again at the clock, back down at the pocket watch, and wonder.

► *Use the clock and the pocket watch to find the answer –*
Turn to the number you discover

(62) # "WHERE TO?"

from 55, 79

"But where to?" Watson calls from behind you.

You stop. In your excitement you hadn't quite worked out where you were headed to next. Watson catches up with you.

"Perhaps as well as matching the arrangement of the letters and hieroglyphs, this pattern is a message," you theorize. "A number code."

"So we're trying to find a connection between the number code and the room numbers on the floor plan," Watson hazards.

"Closely reasoned. You scintillate, Watson!" you exclaim, pulling the map out of your pocket again.

"I say, look at your feet, Holmes," says Watson. There are two small vertical crosses chalked on the ground.

► *Turn to 20*

THE GREEK ROCKS?

from 58, 83, 108

There are some arrows on the floor at your feet, this time with only one arrowhead, pointing in one direction. The message seems simple.

"See, Holmes, these arrows point here," Watson says, tapping at the map. "Exhibit 67."

But then you remember a reference to the 'Greek rocks' in the letter from Bonaparte.

You take out the letter to have another look. "By the Greek rocks, count the cards and repeat your bet."

```
My esteemed genius Mr Holmes and his
foolish friend,

    Buona sera. If you're reading this I know you
have tumbled headlong into my trap. You are my
prisoners for the night. Genius, did I say? I
caught you pretty easily, like a silly wee bird.
    In any case, what kind of genius would be stuck
for so long over the Conk-Singleton papers I laid
in your path?
    Would you say you were an anarchist, Mr Holmes?
A hater of authority? A violent man? By the time
this night has ended I predict you will be seen
in that light by the powers that be. Even by your
brother. You will be shamed.
    You sent my brilliant friend, my inspiration, to
his death. That struggle was in a high place. But
this one will end in profondità.I am preparing for
you the lingering death of imprisonment.
    Gather your papers, Sir, and play the game.
By the Greek rocks, count the cards and repeat
your bet. Prepare to go down, even into
underground realms.
    I wish you buona fortuna. You have until
morning. By then you will either be free or
tangled even more deliciously in the trap I have
laid for you.

---- Bonaparte
```

"What do you think, Watson?"

"Well, the Greek rocks are without doubt the Elgin Marbles... My suggestion," Watson says, "is to count the number of information cards beneath the display of Elgin Marbles and repeat the number. Then go to that room on the floor plan. Simple enough."

"Or we could follow the arrows? Sometimes you don't have to complicate matters. Sometimes simple is correct."

▶ *Follow Bonaparte's clue – Turn to the number you discover*

▶ *Follow the arrows – Turn to 67*

(64) GETTING LATE?

from 101

Watson taps your elbow and pulls you to your feet.

"I dropped off, old man. I know you weren't asleep," he says, good-naturedly, "you were just concentrating very deeply. Anyway, the cleaner came and woke me before dashing off."

Can you have fallen asleep? There was a strange odour in the room. Perhaps you were drugged...

You are suddenly terribly aware of how late it is, or must be. This hidden conspiracy seems to be heading towards a murder planned for the morning. How long do you have left? you suddenly wonder. If only you or Watson had a pocket watch...

Then Watson puts a finger to his lips. You stand stock-still and listen.

▶ *Turn to 88*

221B BAKER STREET

from 50

"Well, Holmes, you outdid yourself there." Watson smiles cheerily from across the room. He sips at Mrs Hudson's tea and nibbles a scone.

"*The* woman provided a little help," you murmur.

"Indeed, yes," Watson says.

You have sent a heartfelt letter to Mrs Norton offering your thanks. You look again at the morning paper. There is no mention of the former Irene Adler's role in foiling this dastardly plot. Perhaps a letter to the editor is needed to set that right...

THE END

The Daily Gazette

KING EDWARD VII SAVED BY SHERLOCK HOLMES
Master Detective Foils Anarchist Plot to Kill King in British Museum Underground
ANARCHISM INFECTS HIGH SOCIETY
Lord and Lady of the Realm in Handcuffs

Is this Sherlock Holmes's greatest triumph? The Baker Street maestro foiled a daring plot to assassinate King Edward VII at an official event in the British Museum Underground Station this morning. Lady Arabella Conk-Singleton – now unmasked as escaped Italian anarchist Bella Rabia – was arrested at the site with her husband, Lord Crispin Conk-Singleton and British Museum assistant director Sir Alisdair Stuart.

Colonel Sebastian Moran, one-time associate of the late Professor Moriarty, was also captured red-handed as he prepared his weapon, and taken into custody.

The arrested individuals – all members of the Bonapartist anarchist group – had plotted to shoot the king dead, but Holmes and his trusty assistant John Watson, MD, uncovered the plot and saved the day.

ROSETTA STONE A FORGERY

The Rosetta Stone on display in the British Museum is a fake. Anarchist plotters hired a skilled stonemason to create a replica and carried off the original, planning to sell it to a wealthy Texan.

The original stone has been found in London Docks and will be returned to the Museum.

The Stone, inscribed in three languages is a key artefact used to decipher Ancient Egyptian hieroglyphs and was found in Egypt in 1799.

(66) A MOMENT'S DOUBT

from 84

"Holmes, old chap," Watson says, looking at the map, "that doesn't look right to me."

"No, no," you say, peering closely at the maze. "I'm sure..." You gesture to Watson. "Come on, old chap, it's just through this doorway."

Watson stands still.

"I think it might be best if I take charge. Follow me," Watson says.

▶ *Follow Watson – Turn to 77*

▶ *Stick to your guns – Turn to 42*

(67) LAUGHABLE

from 63

You are now standing at the other end of the Elgin Room. A frieze faces you. The person on it, a soldier, appears to be laughing. You look around for a clue, a note, a message, but nothing. Just you and the laughing man.

Do you hear a soft laugh somewhere in the silence of the gallery? You look quickly but you can't see anyone.

Something doesn't feel right.

"I can feel them laughing at us," you say, turning to Watson.

"Let's head up to the Phigaleian Room, Holmes," Watson says encouragingly, setting off up the gallery.

▶ *Turn to 33*

(68) ANOTHER MESSAGE

Could there be something in the information cards beneath the Elgin Marbles? There are three cards. The card on the far left has been covered up with another card. It displays a collection of numbers, hieroglyphs and Greek letters:

5 δ 🦅 13 8 δ 21 🐿 🐿 15 7 δ 5 α δ

You decode the message using the Translation Device and make a note of the colour that matches the final letter.

▶ *If the colour revealed is yellow – Turn to 58*

▶ *If the colour revealed is blue – Turn to 83*

▶ *If the colour revealed is green – Turn to 108*

(69) LOOK DOWN

It feels odd to be re-entering a room you escaped only moments before. Watson grips the two maps tightly in his hand.

"All these extra markings, Holmes," he says, turning to you, "they seem to be on the right-hand side of the room. Perhaps some of these bookshelves...?" Watson starts pushing at the bookshelves, but to no avail.

You wander over and lift the map out of his hand. "See, Watson," you say, "they are slightly set back from the wall. More like here."

You take a step to your left and metal clangs beneath your feet. You look down to see a floor grate directly beneath you.

Watson steps over.

▶ *Turn to 44*

You feel something hitting against your leg as you move nervously about in the room. You reach down and find an envelope inside your coat pocket.

"A letter," you say, wondering how it got there. "The cleaner! He must have slipped it into my pocket when he brushed past me earlier."

> *My dearest Sherlock,*
>
> *You tried to help me once, and now it's my time to help you.*
> *These dials need four numbers, from four people. Each dial has a symbol. Look at the symbol and find the person who resides there. You'll have met each of them tonight. Each of these people is known by a code. The number in this code is the dial's position. As for the knobs, well, I've already told you.*
> *I know you often work from the end to the beginning, but this time you need to go from top to bottom.*
>
> *Yours,*
> *JEAN*

"A letter is all well and good, but what does it mean? How do we get out?"

"Let's look at your notes, Watson. I think we're going to need them."

You set your Translation Device to the letter 'M'.

Add the first two numbers together and take the direction of the top knob. Turn your wheel as many places in this direction.

Add the last two numbers together and take the direction of the bottom knob. Turn your wheel as many places in this direction.

▶ *If the colour revealed is green – Turn to 50*

▶ *If the colour revealed is blue – Turn to 60*

TRUSTEES' ROOM

Sir Alisdair Stuart, the assistant director of the British Museum, is lying on his back on the floor. He is panting heavily and appears to be dying.

Poison? you wonder.

Watson inspects him. You edge closer. You see the recognition in Sir Alisdair's eyes when he notices you. A look of excitement seems to pass over his face, but it's just a glimmer. He closes his eyes and sighs deeply.

Sir Alisdair slowly lifts his hand and places it over his breast pocket. You see some papers sticking out beneath.

You surreptitiously take them. Sir Alisdair seems to nod his head.

A doctor hurries in. Watson and the doctor have an intense discussion of medical matters. You examine the documents more closely.

▶ *Turn to 110*

A WORD FROM THE ATTENDANT

You wonder how you might get back into the Museum to continue your research. You pass through the main gates and look up at the night sky.

Watson is at your elbow, pointing. "Look, Holmes! You can see Venus tonight. The goddess of love and beauty. Rather beautiful, isn't she?"

You barely hear him. Your mind is in the Museum, turning the case over. As turn to look at the Museum one last time, the same burly attendant with tiny spectacles appears from the shadows.

"Mr Holmes, Dr Watson," he says in a low voice. "Can I ask ye to step into the forecourt. Och, the strangest thing has occurred. Your additional eye might help us find some solution to this mystery."

Still something about him doesn't seem quite right. You note his strange use of the word 'additional'.

The intrigue gets the better of you. You step into the shadows of the Museum's forecourt.

▶ *Turn to 9*

CENTRAL NORTHERN LIBRARY

You look appraisingly around the Central Northern Library. Bookcases line the walls, and a few open texts lie on a table in front of you. Watson strides to the history shelves.

"I say, Holmes, look at this."

"Watson," you say, looking at the shelf category, "what are you doing looking at books on Ancient Egypt?"

"Not that, Holmes," Watson guides your eye. "They have been playing around with the books."

A number of books have been turned upside down. Counting from the left, the third, fourth, sixth, tenth and eighteenth books have been inverted.

"D'you suppose someone's left us directions in the form of a number sequence?" Watson murmurs.

"Brilliant as ever, my dear Watson."

What's the next number in this sequence: 3, 4, 6, 10, 18...?

▶ *If you're able to break the code – Turn to the number you discover*

▶ *If you're unable to break the code – Turn to 82*

TUNNELLING EAST

You turn east.

"I do rather wish we were walking towards a rising sun," Watson says.

You can feel his morale dipping.

"Not long now, old chap," you cheer him on. "We've got light, we've got this tunnel, what else could we need?"

You lift your hand to pat him consolingly on the shoulder.

Just at that moment, the candle fizzles out, plunging you both into pitch blackness.

"At least that provided a little light relief," Watson commiserates as you both grope your way forwards through the darkness.

▶ *Turn to 38*

⑦⑤ GUIDED BY THE ATTENDANT

The attendant pauses outside the Director's Office and pulls out a chain of keys. He begins searching through them methodically.

You notice something out of the corner of your eye. You turn, and think you see a chap with a broom moving back into the darkness. You blink again, but nothing.

In front of you is a beautiful statue of Venus. It seems to have been moved from its correct position.

"I say, Holmes, is there something significant about this?" Watson asks.

The item code VEN7.DRT has been circled in pencil with the letters IAN written below.

You take note of the code in the notebook, hoping that it might prove useful later.

▶ *Turn to 112*

ARE YOU SURE?

Watson examines the map.

"I can't see 76 on the map, Holmes. Are you sure that's the right answer?"

"Hmmm."

"Have you had a look at the Reading Room ticket?" Watson asks. "That seemed to have some similar symbols on it. Maybe that's the first part of the sequence."

▶ *Go back and look at the sequence – Turn to 7*

▶ *Head towards Room 76 – Turn to 42*

FLYING HIGH?

from 66, 84

You follow Watson through Vase Rooms 2, 3 and 4. He was right, there are a lot of vases. You are beginning to feel a little agitated. There are no clocks, but you have the sense that time is running out. At least it's still more or less night outside.

You arrive in the Bronze Room. The statues glint mysteriously in the moonlight. Then, just for a moment the same light illuminates a face in the darkness. You are convinced it is that handsome cleaner.

"Hello?" you call, but there is no response.

"Come on, Holmes," Watson scoffs, "there is no one here!"

You shake your head, he must be right! It was just a trick of the light. You look to the centre of the room and see what appears to be a small boy stood in the walkway. Another sculpture out of place.

What can this mean?

Watson walks over. "Object ICA.0WQ, a statue of Icarus."

"The boy with waxed wings who perished because he flew too close to the sun," you muse. "I feel a little as though we are flying too close to the sun, Watson."

"What do you mean, old chap?" Watson asks. "It's still night outside, there is no sun in the sky!"

"We're running out of time, Watson. To stop the regicide. We're cutting it fine."

"There are a couple of those hieroglyph markings and symbols scrawled on the floor here," Watson says, pointing to your feet. "Perhaps they'll tell us where to go next."

He leans closer. "There's an IAN here, too. What do you think that can mean?" he says, taking note of the object code for safekeeping.

"No time, Watson, dear chap!"

You pull the Translation Device from your pocket and set about decoding the hieroglyphs. Your heart beats a little faster in your chest.

▶ *Turn to the number you discover*

I AM CONFIDENT

"Fear not, Watson. While we have a chance, I am confident."

"Of course you are. But why does she give us a chance if what she really wants is to keep us out of the way?"

"As she says, she respects my – I mean, human – intelligence. Many anarchists are humanists, after all."

"I think she really wants to defeat you – to humiliate you," Watson says. "She has you where she wants you. And she is teasing you with the possibility, the impossible chance that you will be able to stop her committing this dastardly act."

Where to now? You look at the floor plan.

It looks like a choice of back the way you came; right to the Southern Egyptian Gallery; or left to the Northern Egyptian Gallery.

"Another choice!" Watson says despairingly.

Are there any clues in the letter, you wonder, as to which way to turn?

▶ *Head right – Turn to 45*

▶ *Head left – Turn to 85*

LADY ARABELLA'S LETTER

You see a connection with the letter.

"I propose," you say, "that the pattern on the front of the Museum deliberately echoes the arrangement of the hieroglyphs and letters in the message."

"Ah – 3 in column one, 1 in column two, and so on."

"There's intelligence at work," you say. "We have to go back in."

You stride off across the courtyard. A tingle spreads through your fingertips. This is just getting interesting.

You hear Watson puffing and panting behind you.

"Do you know, I'm inclined to agree with you," he calls.

▶ *Turn to 62*

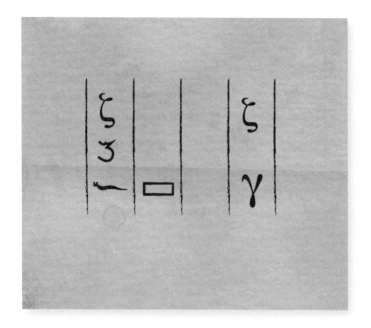

ⓐ⁸⁰ "A ROOM FULL OF VASES"

"We're going up, it appears, Holmes," Watson says, looking at the map.

He leads you up the staircase, along the North Gallery and into Vase Room 1.

"Here we are, a room full of vases! In fact," Watson says, "there are four of them. Who on earth has use for quite so many vases?"

The room is dark, and you move about slowly, trying to get your bearings. As you edge towards the wall, you feel something stop you in your path. Your hand reaches down and you find a long piece of string.

"Here, Watson," you say, calling him over. "It's a piece of string."

"Well, let's follow it, old man," Watson offers, "see where it takes us."

▶ *Turn to 84*

LOOK BEHIND YOU

You turn around and notice something on the ground.

At your feet sits a pair of kitchen scales.

On one side there are seven letters – V, K, S, V, H, F, H – written on separate pieces of card. The other side is empty.

"Hmm. I wonder what this can mean, Watson?"

You both consider the matter for a few minutes.

"What should scales do, Holmes?"

"Balance, I would say."

"And how could you balance a set of letters?"

As you bend closer you see a note in the same scrawly handwriting as the invitation:

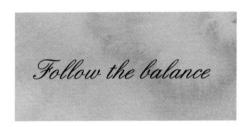

It matches the hand of Lady Conk-Singleton's letter, too. It's all beginning to add up.

Work out the letters that balance those on the scales and spell out a word. Use the numbered map to find the room number that matches that name.

▶ *Turn to the number you discover*

▶ *If you can't work out the letter code – Turn to 95*

COURTYARD GRID

from 73

You can't work out the number code. You sigh. You can almost feel time catching up with you. What time is it now? you wonder. How long until morning and the planned attack on the king?

You wander out into the courtyard to see if looking at the moon will help you gauge the time. It's cloudy. But there are the first glows of colour in the sky. It must be 6 a.m. already, or even 7.

The cleaner appears and hurries over. "This came for you," he says. He hands you a rolled-up piece of paper.

"I say, stop!" you shout. But the fellow has already melted into the shadows and disappeared out of sight.

On the paper is a nine-square grid, along with the words 'Top left, bottom right' and a set of clues:

3 is next to and directly above 9
4 is right of 8 but beneath 1
7 is higher than 8 but lower than 5
6 is next to 5 and directly above 1
9 is above 2 and two squares left of 1

Watson comes over belatedly.

Together, you fill in the grid and take the top left and bottom right numbers to find the next destination on the floor plan.

Hurry, you tell yourself, the king's life depends on it.

▶ *Turn to the number you discover*

from 68

⑧③ WATSON TAKES THE WHEEL

You cannot decode it.

You hand the Translation Device to Watson. You're feeling strangely sleepy tonight.

"Is it something to do with the Marbles, Watson?"

"I think not, Holmes... it points much closer to home."

"What's that?" you ask.

"The regicide is planned against our very own king. It says: Edward VII is dead."

You look down at the Museum floor.

"We must be able to stop this terrible thing happening," Watson says. "It is awful, just awful."

"On the contrary, Watson, it is rather delicious."

"Delicious? What the devil do you mean, Holmes?"

"What time is it, Watson?"

"Don't you have your watch?"

"It's laid out on the operating table at Baker Street. It stopped this morning. I was working on its innards when the letter came and we hurried over here."

"Well, I can't help you. Mine stopped after it got wet in the rain on the way over here. I would guess it must be 9 or 10 at night by now."

▶ *Turn to 63*

⑧④ AMAZE-ING CHALLENGE

from 80

You feel your way along the string in the darkness, and find yourself standing in front of an old Greek vase. You strike a match. There is a glint of light reflecting off something. It makes you think of that attendant's spectacles... And do you glimpse a blurry shadow or a movement in the darkness?

"Did you see that, Holmes?" Watson says. "Is that our fake Scot?"

But you are concentrating on the object the string has led you to.

66   77

"Aha," you say, peering at the glass and smiling. "Very clever! This vase is of Theseus and the Minotaur."

"Theseus who travelled to the centre of the labyrinth to kill the beast, and was led back out by a piece of string!" Watson laughs.

"Hence the piece of string."

"But they've led us in here with a piece of string... Where's the maze?"

"Just here," you say, tapping the information card in front of the vase.

"I suppose we need to work out which number leads us to the centre," Watson offers.

"Quite."

"Just as the next room will lead us to the centre of our puzzle."

"Mmm," you say.

You look at the maze, and decide where to go next.

▶ *Find your answer and turn to it*

You turn left to the Northern Egyptian Gallery. You stride ahead of your companion.

"I think this is the right choice," Watson says, as he follows. "Perhaps 'head upcountry' means go north – to the Northern Egyptian Gallery?"

"Yes, Watson, and wouldn't you say the word 'sinister' was a clue to turn left?"

"Of course! It means left, doesn't it? You're always a step ahead of me, Holmes."

"Only one, Watson?" you fire back.

▶ *Turn to 40*

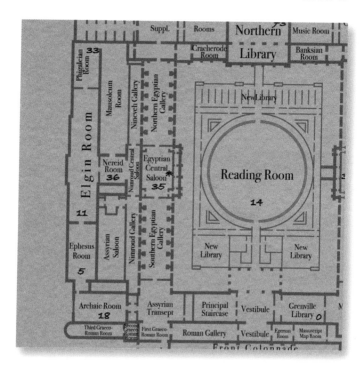

The clock on the wall ticks loudly. You look up – 6.30 p.m.

"I guess we won't make it to the opera tonight then, old chum," you say.

"*Orpheus and Eurydice* this evening," Watson says. "Such a sad story, Holmes. Orpheus who follows his bride Eurydice to the underworld in an attempt to rescue her, and convinces Death to let him, but..."

"We'd better get going. To the Reading Room, it appears."

"Yes. Yes, it does. But hold on a minute," Watson says, "look at this."

On the door frame are some scratched-in hieroglyphs and symbols.

You take out the Translation Device and decode the message into letters.

You aren't quite sure what it means at first, but then you remember that with so many of the best cases, you must begin at the end and return to the start.

You step out of the room, and hear some noise over to your left.

▶ *Follow the noise – Turn to 18*

▶ *Head to the Reading Room – Turn to 23*

PARCHMENT MESSAGE

You approach the door to the Reading Room. It is locked. But there is a roll of parchment propped against it. You unfurl the paper and find the following letters written on it:

GNKLDR ZMC VZSRNM

QDSQZBD XNTQ RSDOR

ENKKNV SGD MNHRD

Another code.

"This fellow seems addicted to coded messages," you say with a sigh.

"Sometimes letter codes like this work by displacement," Watson says. "'A' becomes 'B', 'C' becomes 'D', and so on..."

You ponder.

What does the code say?

▶ *You decode it – Turn to 25*

▶ *You can't decode it – Turn to 54*

DRIP, DRIP

You can hear water dripping, being poured, then dripping again. You look around but there is no movement, just the sound of water. There is something odd about the water's rhythm.

"Holmes, my goodness, Holmes!" Watson seems excited, "I think it's Morse code! I brought notes on the alphabet with me. I've had them since my army days."

You listen closely. The pours must be dashes, and the drips must be dots. You listen closer and hear:

drip – pour – drip
pour – pour – pour
drip – drip – drip
drip
pour
pour
drip – pour

Then the sequence starts again.

Use Watson's Morse code notes (found at the back of the book) to help you decode the message. Then look at the map, and use this clue to work out where to go next.

▶ *You decode it – Turn to the number you discover*

▶ *You can't decode it – Turn to 94*

from 20

You're unsure where to go.

You walk into the Museum and stop in the vestibule, waiting for inspiration to strike. In the fading light you see the burly attendant emerge out of the shadows.

You and Watson duck into the Roman Gallery and crouch down behind a statue.

Will he find you there?

For some reason you want to remain undiscovered.

You hear a rattling of keys over by the main entrance. You stand up in time to see the attendant swing the great door shut, lock it and put away the keys.

"What was that?" Watson whispers rather too loudly.

"We're locked in," you say in a normal voice. You feel a sense of excitement rather than doom.

"Come on," you say, "let's head back to the Egyptian Central Saloon. We can start there."

"I say, Holmes," Watson whispers. The attendant is walking directly towards you.

"Mr Holmes, Dr Watson. What on earth are ye doing there?"

"Edinburgh man, sir?" Watson asks the attendant.

The attendant ignores him.

"This way, please, to the Director's Office."

"Should we, Holmes?" Watson says.

"Come on," you say. "There's only one way out of here and that's to play the game."

The attendant laughs softly.

"Well, if ye're to play the game we should hurry weselves up a little. Did ye not understand the code? With the numbers on the map I thought it plain enough..."

He leads you towards Room 6.

▶ *Turn to 75*

(90) A TWISTED KNIFE

There is a small image with some text scrawled above it, which reads:
Where next, Mr Holmes? What trajectory are we on? To success or failure?
Head to 'x'.

"It's an angle puzzle, Holmes," Watson says. "We'll need to find the
missing one. Angles around a point add up to 360 degrees..."

▶ *Find 'x' – Turn to the number you discover*

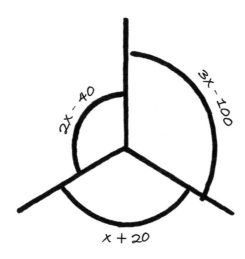

THE LADY ARABELLA

"Most curious, wouldn't you say, Watson?"

"Yes, indeed. I imagine 'the king' is a reference to the Egyptian pharaoh, and 'when he goes underground' to the afterlife? Look for a Stone, it says."

"And what do we know about Lady Arabella Conk-Singleton?"

"Her husband, Sir Crispin, is Mycroft's friend from the Diogenes Club. Unfortunately, as a result, he invited us to their ghastly wedding last year."

"Ah yes, the Italian beauty. You took rather a shine to her, Watson."

He hurries to change the topic. "That was when you had the falling out with Sir Alisdair, was it not? And a certain Irene Norton was there."

"*The* woman," you mutter, looking down.

"And Sir Alisdair was very rude to Mrs Norton."

"What nonsense he was speaking."

"And Lady Arabella – something not quite right about her, Holmes?"

"I am perhaps not an expert on the fairer sex, Watson, unlike you."

▶ *Turn to 37*

RUNNING AWAY

"TWO FLED?"

"Is he taunting us? He thinks we're running away from his challenges?"

"Aha, I have it. It is to do with Shakespeare," you say.

"How the Dickens do you work that out?"

"Look on the back of the invitation. It says 2B/2B. Clear enough, even for you, old man? To Be or Not to Be?"

Your eyes scan the room, and land on the bookcase. *The Collected Works of Shakespeare* is sticking out slightly. You walk over and lift the book off the shelf. It's not a book at all but some sort of secret storage. Inside, you find a blank map of the museum layout, and a ticket for the Reading Room.

▶ *Pick up the blank map – Turn to 106*

▶ *Pick up the Reading Room ticket – Turn to 107*

SOCIETY WEDDING MARRED BY RUMPUS

ANGRY EXCHANGE AT MARRIAGE OF SIR CRISPIN CONK-SINGLETON AND NEW ITALIAN BRIDE, MASTER DETECTIVE SHERLOCK HOLMES INVOLVED

7 June 1900

The society wedding of 1900 was disrupted by angry exchanges involving the great Sherlock Holmes, master detective of Baker Street, and Sir Alisdair Stuart, assistant director of the British Museum. In a lavish ceremony at Westminster Abbey, Sir Crispin Conk-Singleton married his exquisite but little-known Italian bride, now Lady Arabella Conk-Singleton. Afterwards, a dispute broke out during the reception at Sir Crispin's most beautiful St James's Square mansion. Mr Holmes's amanuensis, John Watson, and onlookers including Mr and Mrs Godfrey Norton were seen restraining Sir Alisdair while Mr Holmes laughed long and loud.

► *Examine the other documents – Turn to 110*

from 88

Stuck again.

Watson strides off, humming, and disappears into a room.

"Hello?!" you hear him say.

You hurry in after him, but he is there on his own.

"Quite extraordinary," he says.

You raise an eyebrow.

"That cleaner was here again. She winked at me and asked had I considered visiting central Egypt?"

"She, Watson?"

"He, old man – dreadfully sorry. And then he said to take 13 years from my age to find the place to go."

"You're 48 at present, I believe."

"That's correct."

"So taking 13 away gives you–"

"But how on earth could the cleaner know my age, Holmes?" says Watson, hurrying after you.

▶ *Find your answer and turn to it*

A HELPING HAND

from 81

"Can't make sense of that, Watson."

He is looking at you with a slight smile. "Really, Holmes?"

The rather appealing cleaner emerges suddenly from behind an exhibit, sweeping the floor, and moves towards the doorway to the next room.

"The cleaner seems to be helping us," Watson muses. "See here, Holmes, the 'V' is actually an 'E' and so it is the Ephesus Room."

▶ *Consult the map – Turn to the number you discover*

TUNNELLING WEST

from 44

You turn west.

"Are you sure, Holmes?" Watson asks.

You exhale loudly. You do rather hate it when he questions your work.

"Yes, Watson, I'm sure," you sigh, taking a step towards the west tunnel.

The candle is burning low, illuminating both the wall and the errors in your work.

▶ *Retrace your steps and head east – Turn to 74*

ARE YOU SURE?

Watson examines the map. "I can't see 97 on the map, Holmes. Are you sure that's the right answer?"

"Hmmm."

"Have you had a look at the Reading Room ticket?" Watson asks. "That seemed to have some similar symbols on it. Maybe that's the first part of the sequence."

▶ *Look at the sequence again – Turn to 7*

▶ *Head towards Room 97 – Turn to 42*

FRAMED?

"So we haven't even stopped them?" Watson says. "In fact, we've helped them, and now we'll be framed?" He slumps dejectedly to the floor.

"Let's not give up yet," you say, starting to pace. "There must be some way to find out this code."

▶ *Turn to 70*

⑨⑨ THE MAP

You see a connection with the map.

"Well, what is it?" Watson asks.

"You could read the pattern on the front of the Museum as a set of numbers," you say.

"And?"

"Well, there are numbers on the map, you dolt."

"And?"

You explain slowly. "And, you go to the rooms with these numbers."

You look for the room numbers that match the numbers in the sequence.

▶ *Turn to 55*

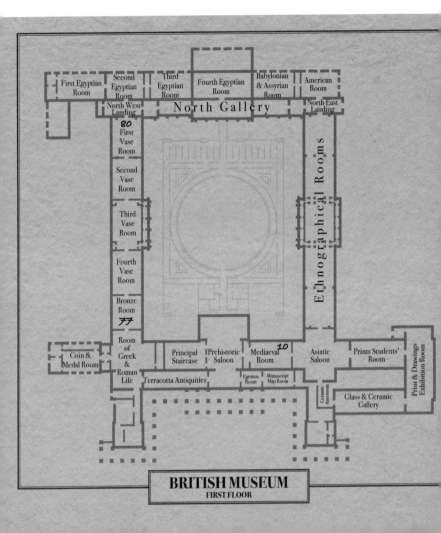

If there is anything of note on the map, write it down in Watson's Notebook.

▶ *Examine the other documents – Turn to 110*

First Egyptian Room | Second Egyptian Room | Third Egyptian Room | Fourth Egyptian Room | Babylonian & Assyrian Room | American Room

North West Landing | North Gallery | North East Landing

80
First Vase Room

Second Vase Room

Third Vase Room

Ethnographical Rooms

Fourth Vase Room

Bronze Room **77**

Coin & Medal Room | Room of Greek & Roman Life | Principal Staircase | Prehistoric Saloon | Mediaeval Room **10** | Asiatic Saloon | Prints Students' Room | Print & Drawings Exhibition Room

Terracotta Antiquities | Egerton Room | Manuscript Map Room | Ceramic Anteroom | Glass & Ceramic Gallery

BRITISH MUSEUM
FIRST FLOOR

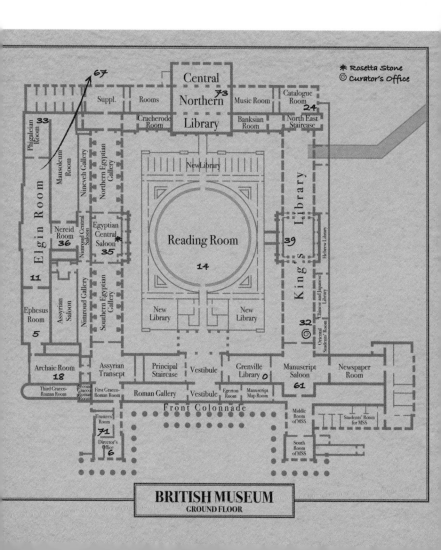

BRITISH MUSEUM
GROUND FLOOR

You sit long-sufferingly. Time is running on, but perhaps Watson can be allowed forty winks.

You don't need to sleep. You never need to sleep when you are on a case – Watson has often remarked on it. This is a chance to run your powerful mind over the case in hand.

You close your eyes.

▶ *Turn to 64*

"THIS IS THE SPOT"

from 38

You are in what seems to be an underground vault. The door bangs shut behind you. A gas lamp illuminates a grate on the far wall, which looks directly onto the tracks and then up to the platform opposite. The platform is hung with ribbons and gaudy banners. You shiver with revulsion. Even in this moment of imminent danger you absolutely cannot stand sentimentality.

Watson walks ahead. "This is the spot," he says, turning to you and miming the action of a sniper's gun. "A bullet shot straight up from here hits that stage perfectly. We've got them."

"I'm afraid, Watson, I rather think they have us."

You point to the floor. There lies a gun, glinting against the flagstones. The pieces fall into place.

"The door handle," he says. "With your fingerprints. We've been framed. We've got to leave."

You turn to the door and are greeted with a large metal contraption, surrounded by curious etchings. There are two knobs, and four dials in a line.

Your curiosity gets the better of you for a moment. "Ah, this is the Singleton Security System!" You turn to Watson. "From the book of patents in the Catalogue Room!"

"Yes, it is." Watson looks around. "But it's also the only door – we're completely locked in."

On the back of the door there is also an envelope addressed to Messrs Watson and Holmes.

Watson picks it up. He opens the envelope, shakes out a letter written in the same scratchy scrawl, and reads: "Well, what can I say? Thank you. You've made this rather easy for us. We'll be joining you soon, on the tracks. But by the time Colonel Moran's bullet lands in the king's heart, there will be no one to find but you, Holmes. In an underground vault. With a gun. With your fingerprints. What a shame. Thank you for playing your small part in the assassination of King Edward VII. You really have been a wonderful help. See you at 9 a.m.! Yours, Bella Rabia – better known to you as Lady Arabella Conk-Singleton."

"Good lord, Holmes! Lady Arabella is the missing anarchist!"

▶ *Turn to 98*

THE FRONT COLONNADE

from 17

"We've escaped, Holmes, we're heading outside!" Watson exclaims.

You follow Watson out of the Grenville Library and into the Front Colonnade. The doors to the Museum are standing open, and in the growing morning light you can see the outline of a figure. You walk forwards.

"Dear Sherlock."

How perfectly dreadful. It is Mycroft. He gives you a superior smile.

"Is the king dead?" Watson groans.

"Fear not," Mycroft says and gives a bark of laughter. "With a little help from Mrs Norton I prevented the attack."

"Oh, thank God he is safe." Watson, of course, is pleased.

You hang your head.

"Mrs Norton...?" you venture.

"Here she is," he says, with a smirk.

The cleaner appears.

"Goodness, what?"

The figure takes off a cap and shakes out luxuriant long hair.

Your heart sinks. And sinks.

Mycroft chuckles infuriatingly. "Née Adler, of course, Holmes."

Irene Adler turns to you. "I was hoping to let the Bonapartist plot run its course so the authorities could catch the anarchists red-handed," she says. "I'd planned that you would be able to find a way to stop the plot yourself. And goodness knows I gave you plenty of hints and clues to help you on your way... But when you failed so signally, I had to alert Mycroft. But the culprits have escaped. I have to say I am disappointed in you, Sherlock."

"Let's get you out of here," Mycroft says with a notable hint of glee. "Looks as though you've got yourself mixed up in some rather unfortunate business."

You open your mouth to speak again.

"No need to say anything now," Mycroft says quickly.

You look at Irene. You can't stand the pity in her gaze.

Mycroft hands you a copy of the morning paper. "Thank goodness one Holmes was on hand to foil the assassination plot," he says, laughing. "I think a knighthood might be on the cards."

THE END

The Daily Gazette

KING EDWARD VII SAVED BY MYCROFT HOLMES

Anarchist Plot to Kill King in British Museum Underground Foiled

LORD AND LADY OF THE REALM IN HANDCUFFS

Sherlock Holmes Humiliated As Leading Government Figure, Brother of the Master Detective, Saves the Day

Is this Sherlock Holmes's greatest humiliation? The Baker Street maestro failed to stop a daring plot to assassinate King Edward VII at an official event in the British Museum Underground Station this morning. The king was saved by leading government figure Mycroft Holmes, the detective's older and seemingly more gifted brother.

Lady Arabella Conk-Singleton – now unmasked as missing Italian anarchist Bella Rabia – was arrested at the site with her husband, Lord Crispin Conk-Singleton and British Museum assistant director Sir Alisdair Stuart.

Colonel Sebastian Moran, one-time associate of the late Professor Moriarty, was captured red-handed as he prepared his weapon, and taken into custody.

Anarchism Infects High Society

As she was taken away, Lady Arabella said: "It should be taken into account that I gave the great Sherlock Holmes many opportunities to prevent this happening. Despite a host of clues laid by myself and my associates, Sherlock failed to stop the plot. Only Mycroft's superior mind was equal to stopping us."

THE AFFAIR OF THE ALUMINIUM CRUTCH

Turn to page 47 to read more about the sensational discovery of a legendary map thought lost forever, and the arrest of its thief, who is now believed to be leader of a rival anarchist group, the Brotherhood of the Red Hand.

(104) A PIPE

from 26, 112

You sit down to smoke a pipe.

Watson is walking up and down in the cramped office, brandishing the piece of paper.

"For goodness sake, calm down."

"How you can be so infuriatingly calm, I don't know," Watson complains.

"Let me have a closer look at the paper."

He approaches and holds it out to you.

Just as he is holding it out, you strike your match.

"Aha," you say, "I thought as much."

▶ *Turn to 16*

(105) THE MISSING NUMBER

from 37

You look at the paper again, and realize that one of your columns doesn't quite add up.

Watson peers over your shoulder.

Your brain clicks into gear.

Before you know it, you are writing '4' into the circled space.

▶ *Turn to 4*

▶ *If you want to check the Reading Room ticket – Turn to 107*

▶ *If you've finished examining the documents – Turn to 48*

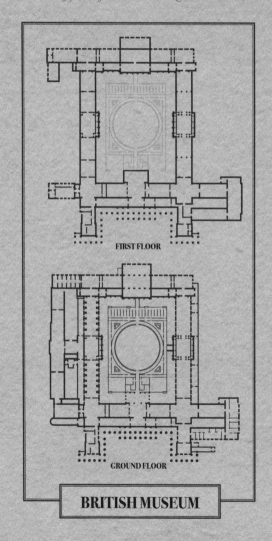

FIRST FLOOR

GROUND FLOOR

BRITISH MUSEUM

READING ROOM TICKET

NOT TRANSFERABLE

THIS TICKET ADMITS

Mr Sherlock Holmes, Esquire

REASON

Research into the Conk-Singleton Case

TO THE **READING ROOM** OF THE
BRITISH MUSEUM

Authorized by Sir Edward Maunde Thompson GCB FBA

Sir Edward Maunde Thompson

A   **B**

▶ *Consult the map – Turn to 106*

▶ *Finish examining the documents – Turn to 48*

A SHERLOCK HOLMES ESCAPE BOOK

WATSON TAKES CONTROL

You cannot decode it.

You hand the Translation Device to Watson. You're feeling strangely sleepy tonight.

"Is it something to do with the Marbles, Watson?"

"I think not, Holmes... It points much closer to home."

"What's that?" you ask.

"The regicide is planned against our very own king. It says: Edward VII is dead."

You look down at the Museum floor.

"We must be able to stop this terrible thing happening," Watson says.

"It is awful, just awful."

"On the contrary, Watson, it is rather delicious."

"Delicious? What the devil do you mean, Holmes?"

"What time is it, Watson?"

"Don't you have your watch?"

"It's laid out on the operating table at Baker Street. It stopped this morning. I was working on its innards when the letter came and we hurried over here."

"Well, I can't help you. Mine stopped after it got wet in the rain on the way here. I would guess it must be 9 or 10 at night by now."

▶ *Turn to 63*

A SECRET COMPARTMENT

from 114

"I hared after him, blowing my whistle as I went. He was fast, but as he pelted round Russell Square, a uniformed figure leapt out from a side street, stuck out a constabulary boot, and tripped him up. It took the two of us to wrestle him to the ground, and clap the darbies on. O'Sullivan eventually caught us up, and gratefully retrieved his crutch. The ruffian was led away, his eyes blazing, but refusing to speak even to protest his innocence.

"I turned to O'Sullivan and asked, 'What was that all about? What is so special about your crutch?'

"He shook his head. 'Hanged if I know, old man.'

"Whipping out the magnifying glass I always carried with me, even then, I said, 'Allow me.'

"O'Sullivan leant against the wall as I scrutinized the crutch. 'Observe,' I said at last, 'this almost imperceptible line. If I press here, and here.'

"There was a faint ping, the line became a gap and I was able to unscrew the crutch-head from its limb. 'Did you know your crutch has a secret compartment?'

"He shook his head once again. 'News to me – look, there's something inside it.'

"We fished inside and pulled out a long, thin cylinder, wrapped in oiled red silk. We unrolled it to reveal a map, bearing the BM stamp."

▶ *Turn to 46*

(110) POISONED MAN'S DOCUMENTS

from 29, 31, 71, 93, 100

While the doctor and Watson are preoccupied, you peruse the assistant director's documents, then pocket them. They are as follows:

▶ *Map of the Museum – Turn to 100*

▶ *Newspaper Clipping 1 – Turn to 29*

▶ *Newspaper Clipping 2 – Turn to 31*

▶ *Newspaper Clipping 3 – Turn to 93*

▶ *A blank piece of paper*

▶ *A Translation Device – see the front of the book*

▶ *If you have finished looking at the documents – Turn to 115*
(Feel free to refer to these documents at any time.)

(111) "IT'S CLEARLY A MESSAGE"

from 0

"It's clearly a message," you say to Watson.
"Come along."

▶ *Turn to 6*

OUTSIDE THE DIRECTOR'S OFFICE

The attendant speaks rather sharply: "Come along, gentlemen, please."
He stands to the side of the door, ushering you through.

At the office door Watson tries to pull you back.

"Holmes, are you sure you trust this man?" he hisses. "He just locked us in the Museum."

"It's not a trap, dear fellow, if we know we're being trapped," you whisper back as you head through the door.

The burly, not-quite-Scottish attendant closes the door behind you.
You are sure there is something in the office that will help you unravel this puzzling mystery – a message or a clue.

Your eyes land on the director's full desk, which makes you wonder about those documents he gave you. As you pull them out of your pocket, the blank piece of paper falls on the floor.

You are struck by it.

"No man just carries a blank sheet of paper around, would you say, Watson?"

You notice a candle burning at the other end of the room.

"How odd," Watson says, "I would have thought they would blow out the candles when closing up?"

You look at the piece of paper, at a loss.

"You could try holding it up to the flame?" Watson says.

▶ *Hold the note up to the flame – Turn to 16*

▶ *Sit down and smoke your pipe – Turn to 104*

ENGLAND'S GREATEST AUTHOR?

from 2

The clue reads: THE BARD.

"The Bard?"

"Shakespeare, one must assume," you say.

"These are really rather simple clues," Watson says dismissively. "He's a little obvious."

"Or she, Watson?" You are wondering about Lady Conk-Singleton and whether she might be connected to the plot.

Watson ignores you. Not for the first time.

"But you're right. Very obvious."

You wish there was a way to know whether Moran, or M. Napoleon, or Bonaparte, or Lady Conk-Singleton, or whoever it is could hear your assessment of their puzzles.

Your eyes scan the room, and land on the bookcase. *The Collected Works of Shakespeare* is sticking out slightly.

You walk over and lift the book off the shelf. It opens in your hand. It's not a book at all but some sort of secret storage.

Inside, you find two things:

▶ *A blank map of the Museum layout – Turn to 106*

▶ *A ticket for the Reading Room – Turn to 107*

MANHANDLED

"One afternoon, O'Sullivan and I happened to leave the Reading Room together, driven out by the snoring of one of the German philosophers who haunt the place – vast beard flecked with sauerkraut, worn-down shoes, ink-stained fingers.

"O'Sullivan's lodgings were in Bedford Place so we walked a little way along together before I ducked into Hook and Pumphrey's bookshop for a browse. I had been in there but a minute or so when I heard O'Sullivan shouting. I dashed outside, and there he was being manhandled by two bearded bruisers while a smaller ruffian danced round them, trying to wrest the crutch away.

"O'Sullivan was fighting them off well, but the odds were against him; you will recollect that I have some repute in the bare-knuckle game, so I leapt into the fray and we soon saw them off. However, the little one seized his chance to snatch up the crutch and took off with it."

▶ *Turn to 109*

THE BACK OF THE MAP

Just as you are folding up the map, you notice a short message scrawled in a messy hand.

It appears to be written in that confounded code again!

You peer a little closer at the Translation Device and realize that in fact it makes use of these symbols. If you put a hieroglyph or symbol into the input box, you get a letter, a number and a colour in return.

You set about translating the message.

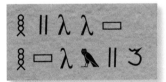

▶ *If the last letter is 'S' – Turn to 51*

▶ *If the last letter is 'Z' – Turn to 59*

GRENVILLE LIBRARY

You head towards Room 0 on the map – the Grenville Library.

You push open the heavy door to find the room in darkness, with six candles in candlesticks placed in a perfect circle on the floor.

"This is a remarkable pleasure," Watson murmurs.

"What's that?"

"Thomas Grenville's library, Holmes, contains the Gutenberg Bible and part of the 1525 edition of Tyndale's New Testament."

"Can't see much here. Do you think these candles are another message?"

"There's a modern Bible here on a table open at the Book of Joshua. What d'you think that means?"

"Another counting challenge, Watson... Counting from the start of the Bible, what number is the Book of Joshua?"

"The sixth."

"And how many candles are on the floor?"

"Seems rather obvious, Holmes. Perhaps you're getting carried away. I'm not at all convinced that this is a message."

▶ *If you think it's a message – Turn to 111*

▶ *If you don't think it's a message – Turn to 57*

HiNts

aNd

SOLutIoNS

221A - HINTS

(2) The Attendant's Identity
The underlined letters in the Diogenes Club invitation spell the word 'place'. Think about the place each letter has in the alphabet and what number would be assigned to that place. Could this be a way to decode the message?

(5) Ephesus Room
Try finding ratios between pairs of the numbers that have been chalked on the floor. Can you then use these ratios to find what all the numbers can be divided by?

(7) Looking for 7
What about the Reading Room ticket (107) you found in the Director's Office – could that help? When you have it, think through the full sequence: A - B - C - D. Which of the bottom images is 'E'? Consider the two ways the image is changing: one movement and one addition. What happens if you make both of those changes happen one more time?

(10) The Men of Lewis
The riddle tells you that: 'The crown, we know, is soon to die, and from behind comes the attack.' This suggests that the king's attacker is behind him. Who is behind the king?

(13) Back
Write out the underlined letters on the information card. Where do they direct you towards?

(14) Reading Room
Look around the room. Can you spot the hieroglyph in different sizes?

(16) Bonaparte
Write down the bold letters in Bonaparte's note. Do they tell you where to look next? Perhaps you need to rearrange them.

(18) **Archaic Room**
Try writing '18' on a scrap of paper and holding it up to a mirror.
What number do you see?

(20) **Coded Choices**
Look for clues in your surroundings that might suggest what to do with
the numbers. Perhaps you've also received some clues in what people have
said to you this evening.

(33) **Triangulation**
Look for triangles nested in other triangles. With a nested triangle, you
need to count both the inside triangles and the outside triangle to get the
correct number.

(34) **Music Room**
Think about the first letter of each image. What word do they spell?

(35) **Rosetta Stone**
Look closely at the item code for the Rosetta Stone. What happens if you
subtract the first part from the last?

(37) **Lady Arabella's Maths Challenge**
Work out what each column, row and diagonal should add up to by finding
the one that is already full. If you get stuck, think about where the remaining
numbers can't go.

(39) **King's Library**
Identify the bold and the red letters in the note, then unscramble these
letters to find two names. You've heard of both of these individuals in
this book. How do these individuals travel? You should find a symbol that
represents this in the room. Some are 'down', others 'up'. How many are
there of each? Put these numbers one after the other.

40 The King's Head

Look on the floor to find the direction the statue is now facing. Use the Translation Device to help you identify where to head to next.

43 Whistle while you Work

To translate the musical notes into letters, you need to think both about how many notes there are in each grouping, and which line those notes lie on. It might help if you number the lines on the musical stave from the top to the bottom. If one musical note on the first line is 'A', and four notes on the fourth line is 'S', how can you connect notes and lines to decode the message?

44 Going Underground

Use your Translation Device to decode the message. What do the symbols spell out in letters?

61 Tick-tock

How wrong is the clock? Work out the difference. If you're unsure what order the digits should go in, have a look at the note and follow the order there.

63 The Greek Rocks?

Look closely at the illustration of the Elgin Marbles (11). How many information cards can you see? Count them up and repeat that number.

68 Another Message

Use the Translation Device to write the symbols and numbers as letters.

70 Help

Irene Adler Norton (IAN) has left you clues around the Museum directing you towards some items you should take a closer look at. Use the stories about these items along with their item codes to connect each drawing to a number to open the door.

(73) **Central Northern Library**
Consider the gaps between the numbers. Is there a sequence there?

(77) **Flying High?**
Use the Translation Device to decode the message. What room might the decoded message be directing you towards?

(78) **I am Confident**
Look closely at Bella Rabia's letter (8). Has she left you any clues about the right direction to head in?

(81) **Look Behind You**
'A' and 'Z' would be perfectly balanced, as would 'M' and 'N'. What letters do you need to balance the ones already on the scales? Where do these letters tell you to go?

(82) **Courtyard Grid**
Put numbers in at the boundaries first – two places above or below another number, or two places to the left or right.

(84) **Amaze-ing Challenge**
Try working backwards. If you start at the centre, what entrance do you end up at?

(86) **Door-frame Message**
Use the Translation Device to decode the message on the door frame. If it doesn't make sense, perhaps try starting at the end and returning to the start.

(87) **Parchment Message**
There are few three-letter words in the English language, so they can be useful in helping you to 'break' codes like these (called ciphers). See if the three-letter words in the code are either 'AND' or 'THE'.

(88) Drip, Drip

Use Watson's notes on Morse code (found at the back of the book) to help you decode the message. Replace the pours with dashes, and the drips with dots. When you've found the word, use the map to see where this item is and head there.

(90) A Twisted Knife

The three angles all sit around a single point, which means they add up to 360 degrees. Form a sum and use this to work out what 'x' is.

(115) The Back of the Map

Use the Translation Device to decode the message.

Cover

The cover design is based on the Sutton Hoo helmet, discovered in 1939 in East Anglia and excavated by a team led by an archaeologist from Cambridge University. We found his name rather interesting.

221B – SOLUTIONS

(2) The Attendant's Identity

The Diogenes Club invitation includes the code: $20 - 8 - 5 / 2 - 1 - 18 - 4$
To decode the message you need to connect each number with a letter.
The underlined letters in the invitation spell out the word 'place', which is
telling you to take each number to represent the place of a letter in
the alphabet.

The twentieth letter in the alphabet is 'T', the eighth is 'H', the fifth is 'E',
the second is 'B', the first is 'A', the eighteenth is 'R', and the fourth is 'D'.

So the code in the invitation spells out the phrase: THE BARD.

(3) The Translation Device

To solve the puzzle you need to put each letter into the Translation Device to
get a sequence of numbers.

'R' translates as 8, 'S' translates as 7, 'F' translates as 12 , 'O' translates as
10, 'R' translates as 8, and 'G' translates as 6.

This gives the sum $8 + 7 + 12 + 10 + 8 + 6$, which equals 51. If you add these
digits together, you get the sum $5 + 1$, which equals 6.

(5) Ephesus Room

To solve this puzzle, you need to find the smallest number (after 1) that will
divide equally into two of the numbers.

If you start with the numbers 145 and 87, you will get a ratio of 5:3.

You can then use this ratio to find out what both numbers are multiples of, by
dividing 145 by 5, and 87 by 3. This gives you 29. All of the other numbers
can be divided by 29 too, so the answer is 29.

29 is an odd number, so you should go forward to the Elgin Room.

(7) Looking for 7

The beginning of the sequence is on the Reading Room ticket (107) found in the Director's Office. Between each element of the sequence the image rotates 90-degrees clockwise, and an extra triangle is added to the left of the shape. This is what we see in square 39, so 'E' is 39.

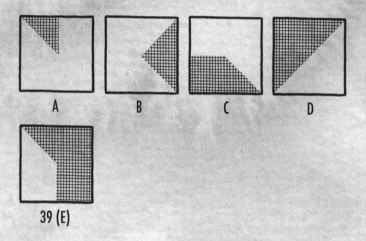

A   B   C   D

39 (E)

(10) The Men of Lewis

The knight is behind the king, meaning that the knight is the killer.

When you put the first and last letters of 'knight' into the Translation Device, 'K' translates to 1 and 'T' translates to 4.

The solution is 14.

(13) Back

The underlined letters in the information card spell out the words 'Elgin Room', which is Room 11 on the map, so the answer is 11.

(14) **Reading Room**
The symbol appears 7 times.

(16) **Bonaparte**
Once unscrambled, the letters in bold type spell out the words 'look on the desk'.

(18) **Archaic Room**
The reflection of 18 is 81.

(20) **Coded Choices**
Earlier, either the Museum attendant or the doctor used the word 'additional'. You also took note of some chalked crosses on the floor, which looked like addition signs. Putting these two clues together suggests you should add the four numbers you see on the Museum's columns (9).

This gives you the sum: 3 + 1 + 0 + 2, which equals 6.

33 Triangulation

There are 12 triangles,
so the answer (12 x 3) is 36.

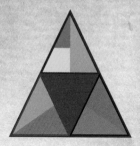

34 Music Room

Taking the first letter of each image spells out: C-A-T-A-L-O-G-U-E,
directing you towards the Catalogue Room, which is Room 24 on the map.

35 Rosetta Stone

The hieroglyphs translate as: NO GODS, NO MASTERS.

The last part of the item code is 9 and the first part is 1, so the answer
(9 - 1) is 8.

37 Lady Arabella's Maths Challenge

The completed square is as follows, giving you the answer 4.

8	11	14	1
13	2	7	12
3	16	9	6
10	5	4	15

221B - SOLUTIONS CONTINUED

(39) King's Library

The bold and red letters in the note give you two anagrams. Unscrambled, the anagrams spell out 'Mercury' and 'Hermes'. Mercury and Hermes are winged messengers, as discussed earlier in the book.

The message tells you that 'Some come flying down below, others keep their secrets up on high.' This references the downturned and upturned wings on the balcony.

If you follow the hint 'Count Holmes' and count the downturned wings first, then the upturned wings, then put the numbers together in that order, you get the answer 32.

(40) The King's Head

By using the compass chalked on the floor, you can see that the statue is now facing South West (SW).

Using the Translation Device, 'S' translates as 7 and 'W' translates as 3, so the answer is 73.

(43) Whistle while you Work

Starting at the top of the stave, a single note on the top line is 'A', one on the second line is 'B', and so on until 'E' on the fifth. Then two notes on the top line is 'F', and so on (as shown in the table below). The notes spell out the words: SIXTY ONE.

Line	1 note	2 notes	3 notes	4 notes	5 notes	6 notes
1	A	F	K	P	U	Z
2	B	G	L	Q	V	
3	C	H	M	R	W	
4	D	I	N	S	X	
5	E	J	O	T	Y	

(44) Going Underground

When decoded, the message reads: 'Go where the sun rises'.

The sun rises in the east, directing Holmes and Watson down the tunnel facing east.

(61) Tick-tock

The difference between 6:30 and 8:31 is 2 hours and 1 minute.

The note says, 'Minutes pass by, we sit and watch the clocks. Hour by hour they tick,' indicating that you should place the minute before the hour, so the answer is 12.

(63) The Greek Rocks?

In the illustration of the Elgin Marbles (11) there are 3 information cards, so the answer is 33.

(68) Another Message

When decoded, the message reads 'Edward VII is dead'.

Entering 'D' into the Translation Device reveals the colour YELLOW.

(70) Help

You have been collecting item codes while you've been in the British Museum. Each of these codes represents a figure, and each figure is part of a story.

IAN pointed you to four items: Venus, the Roman goddess of beauty, is also a planet in our solar system, and had item code VEN7.DRT; Icarus, the boy who perished from flying too close to the sun with his waxen wings, had item code ICA.0WQ; The Nereids, personification of the waves, had item code NER.1RE; and Eurydice, lost forever to the underworld, had item code HEUR.3TY.

The planets at the top of the door correspond to Venus and number 7. The sun and wings correspond to Icarus and number 0. The waves correspond to the Nereids and number 1. The flames of the underworld correspond to Eurydice and the number 3. When read top to bottom, the code is 7013.

Irene Adler Norton, as the cleaner, also told you which way to turn the knob: top left, bottom right.

Starting at 'M', you turn your dial first 7 then 0 places to the left, then 1 place followed by 3 places to the right. This will reveal the colour GREEN.

(73) Central Northern Library

The upside-down books give you the number sequence: 3, 4, 6, 10, 18. The gaps between the numbers form a new sequence, telling us what to add to the last number to get a new one.

The 'gap' sequence is 1, 2, 4, 8. Each number is double the number before, so the next number in the gap sequence is 16, and the next number in the number sequence (16 + 18) is 34.

(77) Flying High?

When decoded the message reads 'Meet that which lies between the fifth and the fifteenth'.

The number 10 lies between 5 and 15, so this message is directing you towards entry 10.

Room 10 on the map is the Mediaeval Room. The Mediaeval period was between the fifth and fifteenth centuries, so this is an additional clue.

(78) I am Confident

In her letter (8), Bella Rabia left you a 'sinister clue' telling you to 'head upcountry'. 'Sinister' means 'left', so you should head left to the Northern Egyptian Gallery.

81 Look Behind You

To solve this puzzle you need to balance out letters by their position in the alphabet. A letter one place in from the start balances with a letter one place in from the end. For example, 'V' is 5 places from the end of the alphabet, so matches with the letter 'E', which is 5 places from the start.

Using this approach, spells the word: EPHESUS.

The Ephesus Room is Room 5.

82 Courtyard Grid

The completed square is as follows:

3	5	6
9	7	1
8	2	4

The top-left number is 3 and the bottom-right number is 4, so the answer is 34. (You may have completed the grid with 2 in the bottom-left square and 8 in the bottom-centre square. This does not change the answer to the puzzle.)

84 Amaze-ing Challenge

The route from 77 leads to the centre of the maze.

86 Door-frame Message
The decoded message reads: FSIONEHTWOLLOF, which, when read backwards, tells you to 'follow the noise'.

87 Parchment Message
Each letter has been moved one place in the alphabet, so 'Z' becomes 'A', 'A' becomes 'B', and so on.

Once decoded, the message reads: HOLMES AND WATSON, RETRACE YOUR STEPS, FOLLOW THE NOISE.

88 Drip, Drip
Using the guide to Morse code at the back of the book, and replacing pours with dashes, and drips with dots, you get the following message: ROSETTA, which refers to the Rosetta Stone.

By looking at the map you can see that the Rosetta Stone can be found in the Central Egyptian Saloon, which is Room 35.

90 A Twisted Knife
Adding the three angles together gives you: $2x - 40 + x + 20 + 3x - 100$

As these angles are around a point, they should all add up to 360 degrees, giving you the following sum: $2x - 40 + x + 20 + 3x - 100 = 360$. When simplified, this gives you the sum: $6x - 120 = 360$

You can then solve this sum to reveal 'x' as follows:
$6x - 120 = 360$
$6x = 480$
$x = 80$

(115) The Back of the Map

When translated, the code reads: Hello Holmes. The last symbol translates to 'S'.

THE PATENT OFFICE

PATENT NUMBER 003456271

SINGLETON SECURITY SYSTEM

The Singleton Security system is an anti-intruder device. The system is installed as a locking device on doors. To open the door the user needs to know a four-digit code, where each number indicates the position of a cog, and whether to turn each small knob – one at the top, one at the bottom – left or right. The system is highly secure. One wrong attempt at inputting the code from the inside will lock the door permanently, so that it can only be opened from the outside with a master key.

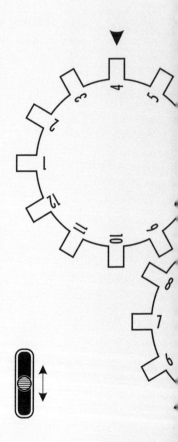

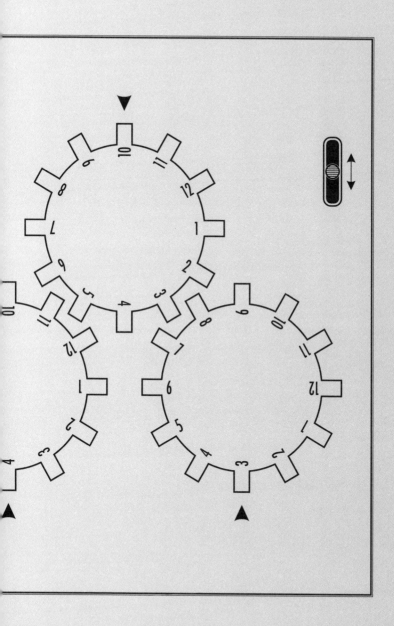

WATSON'S MORSE CODE NOTES

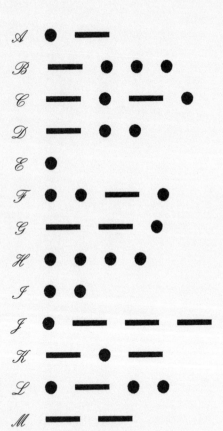

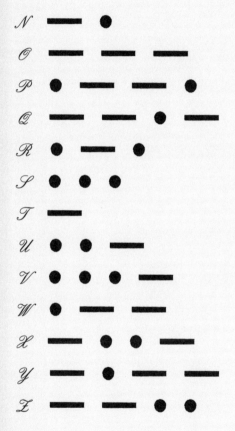

First published 2020 by
Ammonite Press
an imprint of Guild of Master Craftsman Publications Ltd
Castle Place, 166 High Street, Lewes, East Sussex, BN7 1XU,
United Kingdom

Reprinted 2022, 2023 (twice)

ISBN 978-1-78145-420-6

A catalogue record for this book is available from the British Library.

Publisher: Jonathan Bailey
Designer: Robin Shields
Editor: Laura Paton
Additional Text: Viv Croot

Colour reproduction by GMC Reprographics
Printed and bound in China

If you've escaped the pages (or are still trapped!) please
send us a message: **#SherlockHolmesEscapeBook**
@ammonitepress

AMMONITE
PRESS

www.ammonitepress.com